D1590119

The Universe and Mr. Chesterton

p115 – Poetry vs Reason

*p 123 – Buddhism is centripetal – the circle
Christianity is centrifugal – the cross

p150-51 – the good as ought

161 – The optimist and the pessimist

162 – Suicide – ultimate evil

166 – 3 pivotal notions of true philosophy

x 170 – the real trouble with this world of ours – – –

→ 171 – Difficulty of defending what your convinced of – –

177 – Goodness and evil – in beliefs

179 – paradoxes

180-81 – the "fixed point"!

181-2 – progress – liberalism – conservatism

x 183 – cautions against "new" freedoms – – –

188 – pantheism "one thing is a good as another"

x 189 – "God is Love" – explained!

190-91 – ROMANCE

x 199 – "ONLY God and the angels . . ."

205 – the nature of "wonder"

206 – ~~[illegible]~~ ignorance vs falsehood

206-7 – poetry and 209-10

→ 212 – The greatest lesson of all!!! – –

The Universe *and* Mr. Chesterton

+

Scott Randall Paine

Second, Revised Edition

Angelico Press

First published 1999 by Sherwood Sugden & Co.
Second, revised edition published 2019
by Angelico Press
© Scott Randall Paine 2019

All rights reserved

No part of this book may be reproduced or transmitted,
in any form or by any means, without permission

For information, address:
Angelico Press
169 Monitor St.
Brooklyn, NY 11222
www.angelicopress.com

ISBN 978 1 62138 480 9 pb
ISBN 978 1 62138 481 6 cloth
ISBN 978 1 62138 482 3 ebook

Cover design: Michael Schrauzer

CONTENTS

Preface to Second Edition

SHORTLY AFTER World War II, and the atomic trauma of Hiroshima and Nagasaki, an American author published a short book addressed to the public at large; it was entitled: *The Universe and Dr. Einstein.* Lincoln Barnett's slim volume is still considered one of the best short presentations of Einstein's mind-bending theory. That title inspired my own book's title, for reasons it may be worth explaining. The first component of Einstein's theory ("Special Relativity") was promulgated in the opening decade of the 20th century, contemporary with Max Planck's analogous re-reading of nature—this time in the opposite order of magnitude—with the beginnings of Quantum Mechanics. Each theory radically revised the meaning we give to the word "universe." In the vastness of galaxies and light-years, time and space began to look weird, and the solid matter under our feet seemed to start quaking with the buzzing world of atoms. Einstein and Planck went both far beyond and daringly beneath the world of everyday appearances, claiming to find new ways of accounting for what we experience on the deceptive surface of things.

In the same decade that saw Relativity and Quantum theories assail our senses with doubts, at least one contrasting theoretician was also at work. In the face of those two theories' apparently more comprehensive and deeper takes on the world around us—astronomically transcending and abysmally underpinning the surfaces, we were told—this other student of the cosmos had penned a small book of his own. In it, he suggested we to turn our attention in the other direction: *back* to those surfaces. A vista more far-reaching and fundamental than the celebrated disclosures of the new physics was awaiting us there, he proposed. Still, he was writing about the selfsame universe analyzed by Einstein and Planck. Or was he?

His discovery was simple enough: if instead of looking beyond or beneath the world, you returned to your childhood instincts and simply looked *at* it, you might notice once again what every two-year-old still knows, namely: *what the world really and truly looks like.* Greeting it face-to-face with your naked quintet of senses, could it be that instead of being deceived by "appearances," you are in fact being positioned to see the world as it truly is, with its deepest meaning and most seminal message on unmistakable display? Could that meaning and message turn out to reveal something far more intimate than quarks and pions, and far more exalted than pulsars and quasars?

For the author I'm referring to, this natural view of things is the *proportioned* view, the one which only displays its marvels to our senses in their original constellation. A huge optical telescope and a high-resolution microscope may reveal distant grandeurs and infinitesimal mini-structures respectively, but both instruments will have eyepieces of roughly the same size, proportioned to the sovereign human eye, still stationed anatomically in our head. Even the high sophistication of radio telescopes and electron microscopes will only deliver their findings when our eyes of flesh turn to them to scrutinize their readouts. As interesting as the new scientific dimensions undoubtedly are, the world we encounter with our unaided senses, explore by walking about on our two legs, and ponder with a mind custom-made to order images and peer into archetypes—*that world* is the realest world of all for this third author. And the "right view" of that world (the *orthos doxa* in Greek) was the title he thus gave to his little book about eloquent surfaces: *Orthodoxy.* The author, G.K. Chesterton, not only recaptured and defended the common view of the cosmos; he also plumbed its rootedness in metaphysical and moral principles. Never having studied this in technical philosophical literature, he somehow caught sight of it in all literature and indeed all experience. Unlike Nietzsche, whose abyss famously looked back at him as he peered into it, Chesterton suggested that it is the "superficial" universe itself that is looking back at us, and bidding us to return the gaze.

Like Einstein's theory, though, Chesterton's short book (some 150 pages) is not always an easy read. Many will be puzzled by the itinerary of the man's unique style and perhaps dazed by the impact of his steadily unloaded insights. Thus, just as Barnett's book provided Relativity with a sort of primer, the present book renders a similar service in approaching what is probably the most brilliant and seminal of Chesterton's books. It also requires that we approach his thought by taking a philosophical detour. We will need to spend some time pondering the modern philosophers who first fashioned this new, "scientific" approach to the world with which Chesterton wrestled. Often enough, its promoters claimed legitimacy precisely by appealing to the new physics.

Although the insights of Chesterton do not negate or question those of Einstein or Planck, they do keep them at bay, and vigorously deny them the prerogative of robbing us of a prior and more fundamental perspective. This is no small service, for it is this perspective that makes us human. And there is more. The Christian faith he had earlier rejected turned out to be in holy collusion with this proportioned perspective, and in a way that surprised no one more than Chesterton himself. The purpose of the present book—and then, I propose, of *Orthodoxy* itself—is to help us reset our cognitive software and take a new look at the world. We will discover that new look to be an old look, as we gaze again like children at the grandiose spread of reality before us, courtesy of the universe and Mr. Chesterton.

⊕

This second edition has been only slightly revised in order to accommodate a partial change in perspective in my own thinking since penning this text now some thirty years ago. One matter regards the relation between Chesterton's thought and Eastern philosophies. Chesterton died in 1936 and his exposure to the "wisdom of the East" was minimal and even sketchy. It could hardly allow for a proper evaluation of the vast philosophical contributions of India and China. He himself says as much, as I mention in the concluding pages of the second chapter of Part I. Thus, the contrast of his basically Thomistic metaphysical point of view with "Oriental" thought—often enough highlighted in my study—needs to be further nuanced. It has only been since the middle of the last century, well after his death, that more adequate translations of Eastern philosophical texts have become available. Late 19th- and early 20th-century popular versions—a better word may be "pop"—of Yoga, Vedanta, Buddhism and related schools (the sorts that Chesterton encountered), often seemed to suspiciously resonate with certain philosophical trends of the times. Skepticism, relativism, pragmatism, pantheism and especially atheism and evolutionism were typically chaperoned into hastily arranged marriages with the philosophies from beyond the Indus. It was against these hybrid heresies, above all, that Chesterton directed his critiques. Eastern thought, at its best, is anything but unsubtle. Nonetheless, Chesterton's suspicions are well heeded today, since survivals of the superficial theosophies of his time are still very much with us, however much serious scholarship has left them behind.

On another front, some readers of the first edition thought I was unfair to the three modern masters I single out as engineers of the post-classical approach to philosophy. This applies especially to Husserl. I will only point out here—as I clearly did in the text—that I never proposed to engage with their entire philosophical work, or even major parts of it. My intent was only to address their initial *choice* not to begin philosophizing with a prior, uncritical acceptance of the ontological evidence of cosmic existence. What concerned me was how this initial choice impacted where their philosophy *ended up*.

Of course, there is much to learn from all of them, including Descartes. Certainly Kant will continue to be reread and discussed for the foreseeable future. Husserl in particular has been vastly influential in redirecting many contemporary thinkers "to go back to things themselves." Their tutorship under his guidance, however, has borne fruit only insofar as they accepted his initial method of careful attention to phenomena as they are given, and not by following up in his latter obsession with reducing all knowledge to what he calls "strict science." Thinkers such as Edith Stein, the Lublin school of phenomenology, along with the students of Dietrich von Hildebrand, for instance, all have shown how realist employment of Husserl's early methodology can be fruitfully developed.

For the most part, the original text stands as it was in the first edition. Several typographical errors have been corrected, and occasionally slight stylistic adjustments have been made in the interest of readability.

I am pleased that Angelico Press has judged *The Universe and Mr. Chesterton* worthy of a new edition, and, notwithstanding the qualifications mentioned above, I am happy to say that after three decades, my mind still assents and my heart still responds to the arguments presented.

Scott Randall Paine

Introduction

TO HAVE A right view of things is to be orthodox. To be universal is to be catholic. Those, at least, were the meanings these Greek words were born with. And in the Western tradition, a person who endeavored to put the orthodox, catholic view of things into rational, articulate form was designated by another Greek word: philosopher. The fact that Orthodoxy has come to signify the Eastern half of Christendom, and Catholicism, the greater part of the Western half, is surely no accident. Philosophy and Christianity are akin in their deepest resources. Both are about the *Logos* (the Word)—the first considers the *Logos* by Whom the world was made; the second believes in a *Logos* by Whom the world was saved.

It is no secret, however, that the collaboration one would expect between philosophy and Christianity has been rare and troubled in the modern world. As Christendom has been halved, quartered and decimated in denominations with the progress of the centuries, philosophy too has broken off into "sects" of warring schools. Both seem to grow less catholic and less orthodox as time goes on. As a result, Christianity makes less and less sense to the modern philosopher and the modern philosopher's view of the world typically falls out of step with the everyday assumptions of the man in the street.

The Aristotelian philosopher's view was once considered right and universal, at least by many. Aristotle was considered to be a man quite literally in touch with the universe he viewed. In the main he trusted both his senses and his reason to be reliable registers of the real, and encouraged by this confidence, philosophically vindicated the canons of common sense. What moved early Christians to call their faith orthodox and catholic was precisely the way in which the universe with which the common, everyday man was in contact turned out to be touched and transfused with new meaning by Christ. Christ was in touch with man and his world in a way no other religious figure had ever claimed to be. In more ways than one, His Gospel made sense.

Now, our first sense-contact with the world around us, together with our intellect's reaction to it, constitute what Aristotle and Aquinas hold to be the foundation of all human knowledge: the grasp of being. In contrast, most influential modern philosophers have attempted to pursue wisdom without taking that first touch as their point of departure. And not only do they usually end up out of touch with everyone's common experience, but characteristically articulate world-views quite out of reach of supernatural revelation.

These were the conclusions to which G.K. Chesterton came in a small volume published in England in 1908. He quite deliberately entitled the book "Orthodoxy," and it is far from insignificant that fourteen years later he became a Catholic. In the book, he tells the story of how he had discovered an astonishing and radical affinity between common-sense philosophy and the common man's Christianity. The right view of the universe, to which his own philosophical quest had led him, turned out to be uncannily connected with the doctrine taught by Christianity for 2,000 years. And the righter the view became, and the more philosophical its articulation, the more catholic it grew.

The greater part of Chesterton's writings can be understood as so many attempts to recapture a lost common wisdom that once linked in spiritual brotherhood the sage with the saint. But it was in the book *Orthodoxy* that this link was first fully profiled and unambiguously affirmed.

Unfortunately, the man's work has seldom been consulted for these lessons in remedial metaphysics. It is in the service of such a disclosure that the present book is offered. It is only a beginning, but it is precisely the beginnings of thought that are so befuddled today. And Chesterton's message about those beginnings brings us back to that sovereign touchstone of all philosophical reflection: the universe. Chesterton was a spokesman for the common man and his common universe. He came to believe that in God's plan, it is only by touching and viewing that universe that a man becomes orthodox and catholic—both in the original senses of those words, and, for Chesterton, in the ultimate, upper-case sense as well. In the pages that follow, I hope it will become evident how deeply and how surprisingly true this is.

In order to philosophically explore the way first principles are secured, and the epistemological and moral consequences of their betrayal, we shall begin with Chesterton's intellectual crisis as a youth. His eloquent description of how he recovered those principles—and how that recovery saved him from madness—will form a vivid test-case in the matter of principles. In Part I, we shall look at that crisis itself and its issue. In Part II, we shall examine the way three modern philosophers have attempted to avert such crises by forging new principles of their own. In Part III, the philosophical content of Chesterton's *Orthodoxy* will be analyzed as a speculative challenge to any such attempt at originality in first principles. Part IV, finally, will highlight three inalienable features of any philosophy which is true to the first salute of the universe.

Note to the Reader:

Part II can be skipped by those less familiar with technical philosophical discussion. The principal ideas of the book are on full display in the remaining parts.

I

Chesterton and the Western Tradition

"It is the only way," he kept repeating; "it is the only answer to the heresy . . . which is to fancy that mind is all. It is to break your heart. Thank God for hard stones; thank God for hard facts; thank God for thorns and rocks and deserts and long years. At least I know now that I am not the best or strongest thing in the world. At least I know now that I have not dreamed of everything."

~ G. K.C., *The Poet and the Lunatics*[1]

1. THE THINKER

"This is the only final greatness of a man: that he does for all the world what all the world cannot do for itself."[2] With these words, Gilbert Keith Chesterton discerned a cardinal quality of those giants of history he so readily and generously admired. He would never have dreamt of calling himself great, except maybe in terms of inches and pounds. He was too continuously in the presence of creation and its God to be able to regard himself as anything more than an appreciative viewer. But appreciative he was. And if there was greatness in the man, it had in some way to do with his

1. PL, 126. [All quotes from Chesterton will be referenced according to the abbreviations of his works in the Bibliography.]

2. CD, 299.

uncanny gift of appreciation. One is tempted to christen him the Great Appreciator. Indeed, anyone who has read deeply in Chesterton's works might conclude that in the appreciation of reality contained in them, he has done for all the world something all the world seems no longer able to do for itself.

Shelves of books have been written about this man and his writings, and the conspicuous variety of approaches taken is testimony to his many-sided appeal—and to his almost intractable versatility of thought. The first attempt at a Chesterton bibliography had to be repeatedly revised, and the immense task finally turned over to a computer. "There seems to be no end of him," one bibliographer complained.[3] And one of his many anthologists, after laboring over a selection of passages and the composition of an appropriate introduction, remarked that "the difficulty in trying to write anything about Chesterton is that there is so much of him. Any sentence that one writes about him could be expanded into a paragraph; any paragraph into an essay; any essay into a book."[4] The present book, lest it become a library, shall not be occupied except obliquely with the literary side of Chesterton's production, or with his life and times as such; the only exception will be a pivotal period of his youth. For the most part, I shall follow our opening impression regarding his gift of appreciation. I suspect it may lead us to an overlooked source of the man's manifold creation.

There is something incongruous and almost ludicrous about Chesterton's conspicuous and vocal appearance upon the intellectual stage of the early 20th century. In the grave

3. John Sullivan, compiler of the first Chesterton bibliography *G.K. Chesterton: A Bibliography* (London: University of London Press, 1958), a supplement (*Chesterton Continued*, 1968) and a postscript (Bedford, MA: Vintage, 1980).

4. A.L. Maycock, *The Man Who was Orthodox* (London: Dennis Dobson, 1963), Introduction.

and dour climate of the age, in a gallery of thinkers seized with anxieties and sharing black visions, the rotund face of "G.K." beams in suddenly and begins chatting in a familiar and even frolicking manner. It would have been easy enough to brand him as a buffoon, open the opposite door, and let him dance right on through, except for one thing: although everyone was staring at the big man—and with varying degrees of indignation—a few had, almost despite themselves, begun leaning over attentively and listening to what the man was saying. And they were visibly moved. It seemed this unexpected, bibulous visitor was uttering words which sped strangely to the heart. From his mouth came coherent sermons of gratitude in honor of a world over which these more fashionable thinkers were pronouncing doom. There was something new in his tone and style, but something old and hauntingly familiar in his message.

For reasons of his own, this philosophical Falstaff chose the life of a journalist, even turning down a chair of literature offered him at an English university. He spent nearly forty years pouring forth a deluge of articles, poems, novels and works of criticism, history, biography, social commentary, philosophy and Christian apologetics—nearly one hundred volumes and thousands of brilliant essays which saw the daylight of only one daily newspaper.[5] Clearly, in this man, God had unleashed something singular upon the world. All who knew him sensed an undeniable greatness. Even today there is no lack of enthusiasts who break spontaneously into superlatives at the mere mention of his name. Severe intellectual enemies like George Bernard Shaw conceded that they were dealing with a "colossal genius."[6] He

5. See references in Sullivan.

6. Maisie Ward, *Return to Chesterton* (New York: Sheed & Ward, 1952), 4.

was mocked by some, but nobody seemed capable of disliking him. There was perhaps no one as vehemently against everything Chesterton stood for as was H.G. Wells. But even Wells drew consolation from his intellectual foe in the face of the dreaded possibility that the Christian faith might be true after all. He once remarked that the last-minute maneuver of telling God he knew Chesterton would get him into heaven if anything would.[7]

Now if, as is being suggested, Chesterton's greatness had in some way to do with his ability to appreciate, what was it exactly that he so ably appreciated, and what was his preferred means for its expression? When we ask this question, the greatness of the man begins to slip away from us again. He wrote several popular novels and stories, but no one seriously maintains that he was a great novelist.[8] He wrote two or three poems that have been called great, and many that are regarded as quite good, but hardly enough that one would wish to call him a great poet.[9] It is perhaps to be expected that his works of literary criticism will continue to gain deserved attention and a certain greatness in this achievement acknowledged. But the Chesterton enthusiast demurs: when he speaks of "the great Chesterton," he is not talking about a literary critic. His biographies too are of great interest, but as we shall see, not exactly because they are biographies. And although his social and economic writings are currently enjoying renewed assessment and study,

7. This was actually a letter from Wells to Chesterton in 1933: "If after all my Theology turns out wrong and your Theology right, I feel I shall always be able to pass into Heaven (if I want to) as a friend of G.K.C.'s. Bless you." Cited in Ward, 604–5.

8. Ian Boyd, *The Novels of G.K. Chesterton: A Study in Art and Propaganda* (London: Paul Elek, 1975).

9. Aidan Mackey, "The Poetry and the Publishers..." in *The Chesterton Review*, vol. VII, no. 4, Nov., 1981, 294–306.

here again, our accolades are arrested, for one often complains about their lack of concrete practical realism. This echoes again the recurring suspicion that here as elsewhere in his opus, the undeniable light and penetration seem to draw their energies from an endowment in the author's mind that is not per se socio-economic (or whatever the issue at hand), but somewhat deeper and just out of sight.[10]

But surely, one might propose, he was a great essayist? Indeed—but is the genre of the essay adequate material for the impact we must account for? Will it do to say "il est grand dans son genre, mais son genre est petit"?[11] It is the same with his travel books; they, too, are intensely interesting, but it is something other than travel that makes us read them. One of those travel books in particular gives us a clue as to what that might be. In one of the many long digressions in his book on Rome, Chesterton offers a brief apologetic remark which may help us to isolate that elusive wellspring of his genius:

> I know it will be the general impression about this book that I cannot talk about anything without talking about everything. It is a risk I must accept, because it is a method that I defend. If I am asked to say seriously and honestly what I think of a thing . . . I must think about it and not merely stare at it.[12]

Anyone who has read much of the man's work will brighten up immediately at this passage. That, if anything, identifies Chesterton!—a man who cannot talk about anything without talking about everything. His close friend Hilaire Belloc said that "it was not possible for him to hold

10. Margaret Canovan, *G.K. Chesterton: Radical Populist* (New York: Harcourt, Brace, Jovanovich, 1977).

11. See Banshi Dher, *G.K. Chesterton and the 20th Century Essay* (New Delhi: 1977).

12. RR, 217.

anything worth holding that was not connected with the truth as a whole."[13] Ronald Knox agreed:

> I call that man intellectually great, who sees the whole of life as a coherent system, who can touch on any theme, and illuminate it, and always in a way that is related to the rest of his thought, so that you can say, 'Nobody but he could have written that.' Chesterton was such a man. . . .[14]

Now, like it or not, this proclivity for the universal is an ingredient in that special and rare make of mind the world has traditionally termed philosophical. It seems that whatever Chesterton said was somehow hooked up in his own mind with the universe as a whole, and thus bore a philosophical stamp.[15] After his only personal encounter with Chesterton, Etienne Gilson seems to have walked away in a kind of daze, declaring, "Everything he said was an intellectual revelation!"[16] What do you call a journalist who elicits such a response from one of the foremost Thomists of the century?

Some have candidly yielded to the obvious temptation and called Chesterton a philosopher;[17] to which christening other more meticulous observers have understandably objected. They point out that in the ordinary course of things, philosophers devote themselves to philosophical texts and not to literature, write treatises and not poems, novels and essays, and that they are wont to lavish their insights on scholarly journals and universities, and not on daily newspapers and English pubs. Chesterton in fact would loudly applaud such demotions as these, having maintained throughout his life that he was nothing more than a journalist and never intended on being anything more.

13. Appendix, 157.
14. Ibid.
15. CW, vol. XXVII, 126.
16. Letter to Rev. Kevin Scannell, 7.1.66 (private collection).
17. Appendix, 157 ff.

The hosannas continued nonetheless. Even before the middle of his career, two independent "Chesterton Calendars" were assembled by his readers, carefully organized with thoughts of the man for every day of the year.[18] Books bearing titles such as "The Wisdom of G.K. Chesterton," "The Laughing Prophet," and even "G.K. Chesterton's Evangel," began to appear.[19] Many similar tributes could be cited right up to the present day, some seeming to compete in the effort to wed just the right adjective to just the right substantive and thus finally pinpoint the man's greatness: the Wild Knight, the Man Who Was Orthodox, Metaphysical Moralist, Dynamic Classicist, Jester Knight, Radical Populist, etc.[20]

Perhaps the most stunning instance of philosophical bravura was displayed by Chesterton in his little book on St. Thomas Aquinas. The story of the book's birth gives us a glimpse of Chesterton at work.[21] Even admiring friends had feared that the journalist had finally overstepped his competence by daring such a study. Having nary a degree to his name, and no formal philosophical training, Chesterton called his secretary to the typewriter and dictated half the book in one sitting. Predictably hitting upon a certain limit of material stimulation in his still finite memory, he sent her out to procure "some books on St. Thomas." After the befuddled secretary had produced a small stack of volumes

18. *A Chesterton Calendar.* Compiled from the Writings of "G.K.C." Both in Verse and in Prose (London: Kegan Paul & Co., 1911); and *The G.K.C. Calendar: A Quotation from the Works of G.K. Chesterton for every day in the year,* selected by H. Cecil Palmer (London: Cecil Palmer and Hayward, 1916).

19. Patrick Braybrooke, *The Wisdom of G.K. Chesterton* (London: Cecil Palmer, 1929); Emile Cammaerts, *The Laughing Prophet* (London: Methuen, 1937); Sr. M. Virginia, S.N.D., *G.K. Chesterton's Evangel* (New York: Benzinger, 1937).

20. See Appendix.

21. Read Maisie Ward's account: *Gilbert Keith Chesterton* (New York: Sheed & Ward, 1943), 618–20.

recommended by a priest, Chesterton gave them a brief and desultory perusal, after which he called Miss Collins back to the typewriter. Without further delay he dictated the remaining half of the book. According to Miss Collins, the new books were not consulted again. And the manuscript had no footnotes, no critical apparatus, no references—just the flow of Chesterton's thoughts.

The publishers held their breath. Chesterton's many followers would certainly love this book as they loved all his books, but what about the new corps of trained Thomist scholars now stalking the academies, discussing the most abstruse metaphysical and moral issues, and composing tomes sporting immense scholarship and conspicuous cross-references? What will *they* say? The book was published and the Thomists gravely and quietly pored over the rolling, unannotated pages of Chesterton's effortless prose. The eyebrows were raised, but the eyeballs were carefully reading. Suddenly, to everyone's surprise, it seemed as if the pundits had jumped to their feet and broken into applause. Again, Etienne Gilson's comment says it all: "I consider it as being without possible comparison the best book ever written on St. Thomas.... Chesterton was one of the deepest thinkers who ever existed." Gilson repeated and re-emphasized this encomium throughout his life, and other Thomists of the highest authority, like Maritain, Mandonnet and Grabmann, followed suit, with like astonishment, though perhaps with more measured celebration. So here we are again.

We are constrained, therefore, to locate the greatness of Gilbert Chesterton not in any particular genre of writing—and he exercised himself in almost all of them—but in something which was present in all his writing, of whatever kind. And this was quite simply his thought. And what it was about his thought that was great, I insist, was its philosophical depth and keenness.

Now no sooner is this uttered than someone laughs and

tells us not to waste our time. If it is philosophy we want, we can dispense ourselves with bothering at all with Chesterton's unwieldy production and turn to more systematic philosophical writers. After all (we are told), Chesterton himself never claims to offer a philosophy which only he has to give. Quite the contrary, his whole point is that what he presents is nothing more than the perennial philosophy of Western civilization. He insists on being a conduit and not a fountainhead. We could thus chime in with the observation of the critic who wrote many years ago:

> Certainly, if Chesterton is solely valuable as a philosopher, he is operating under a disadvantage that entirely blunts his efforts. Most men do not realize that he is a philosopher (nor did he), and only those who are learned in Thomistic lore seem able to isolate it, to unearth it from Chesterton's mountain of verses and essays. The natural question is: why not read Aquinas and forget Chesterton?[22]

A very good question. And those who have maintained that our author's "rhetoric and verses," and all the "literary and journalistic Chesterton" should be abandoned in order to find the "metaphysical moralist," will find the question difficult to answer.[23] But I propose that the answer to the question is quite simple and obvious: we should indeed read Aquinas rather than Chesterton—but we cannot. We citizens of the modern and post-modern world are unable to read the Angelic Doctor in the only way that he can be properly and fruitfully read, which is in the chorus and context of the Christian culture in which he wrote, and from which his imaginative and mystical life drew their sustenance. There is so very much missing in the minds of even the best of con-

22. Gary Wills, *Chesterton: Man and Mask* (New York: Sheed & Ward, 1961), 4.

23. Hugh Kenner, *Paradox in Chesterton* (New York: Sheed & Ward, 1947), xxi, 1, passim.

temporary Thomists that was all over the mind of the 13th-century Thomas. And it was more than just his reasoning. It is something you cannot get *from* the *Summa*, but something without which you cannot really get *to* the *Summa*.

St. Thomas knew the Psalter by heart. He composed liturgical hymns. He prayed for hours every day. He walked all over Europe. He was surrounded by a rich Catholic culture, imaginatively and physically immersed in the element of the faith, and addressing students who were in the same milieu. It was only against this physical, imaginative and religious background that his severe scientific syllogisms carve their imposing profile. His mind could focus in quite coolly on the outlines of most rarefied argumentation without divorcing his intellect from his heart. But when we try to read Aquinas today without that backdrop, or some decent approximation of it, we run the risk of knowing much about what he says, but nothing about what he is talking about. We will be cutting syllogisms in our intellect against an artificial backdrop of sentimental music, rock-and-roll rhythms and television commercials. In these latter, neo-pagan times, the great Christian philosophers must give more than mere argument. They must give in some way the warmth of the Christian hearth and the inspiration of the Christian heart, or else the arguments of the Christian philosopher are going to echo in a void.

The great value of Chesterton is precisely his fusion of the philosophical with the rhetorical, the imaginative and even the charitable. Perhaps the fullness of these harmonized endowments could best be captured by saying that he possessed an Augustinian imagination, a Thomistic intellect and a Franciscan heart. All that which surrounded Aquinas like a mothering atmosphere, has entered into Chesterton like a fugitive world pursued into a sanctuary. And when the arguments come (and come they do!), that world comes with them and tempers our cogitations with unspoken lessons. Philosophical wisdom is housed in its natural, sustaining medium of the language of common sense, the inner environment of a richly furnished memory, and a heart warm with humor and charity. How much of this has been lost in our cold and melancholy century! If we are to find our way back to the love of wisdom, we must re-establish the matrix of this traditional Western sanity, lest we father unviable cogitations, and be wise guys rather than sages.

I fear this will be easily misunderstood. These qualities Chesterton exemplifies are not mere auxiliary adjuncts in his writing, like stimulating condiments; nor can they even be compared with sugar-coatings. They do help, they do stimulate, and they are, especially in this man, often sweet. But they belong to a higher order than that of mere literary relish. They belong to the man. And for Chesterton, that man thinks best who thinks as a human being, and not merely as a brain. The position and function of the more "vital" elements in the work of philosophizing are, of course, already hoary topics in contemporary thought. But this threatening overgrowth of the merely cerebral and scientific, and its severance from the imaginative and volitional, are dangers that Chesterton pointed out not merely by talking about them, but by exhibiting in himself how their harmonization can be worked. And he saw that the restoration of such harmony constituted for 20th-century man a return. Cogitation dislodged from a full, warm, breathing sensorium of a person seized by sanity, can lead one very far afield indeed. Some seem never to find their way back. Of this we will have to treat at some length in later chapters.

Chesterton's philosophical thought, couched as it is in the imaginative and mystical womb we shall explore, has something of the prophetic call in summoning our wayward minds back to the lost art of fully incarnate reflection. This return is for Chesterton a return home. And the retreat is from a strange and perilous foreign terrain on which he himself had left far too many footprints. We will be unable to discern the uniqueness of Chesterton's philosophical gift of appreciation without drawing into the picture the context of its genesis.

The story is brief and dramatic, for he grew into this gift out of the midst of a crisis. His vivid imagination, his intellectual sagacity, his burning heart and his natural mastery of rhetoric, all were joined and disciplined, not by the rigors of a long and measured academic regime, but rather by the shock of a single thought. He discovered this thought as a quite young man, rolled it around in his head and caught a chilling glimpse of its inner life. And then he fled. He had mentally meandered into the clutches of "the thought that stops all thought,"[24] and found himself rubbing noses with the Father of Lies. That shock dispatched him at once upon an excited and perilous pilgrimage. Chesterton's philosophic intellect must be seen together with the blistered feet of a pilgrim who learned anew, in one quick and bracing lesson, how to appreciate the world his mind had nearly annihilated.

2. THE PILGRIM

The turning-point in G.K. Chesterton's intellectual and moral life occurred while he was a young man of about twenty. Once he made the turn, however, he remained pointed in the new direction till the end of his life—indeed beyond it. A further turn, his conversion to Roman Catholicism thirty years later, was but the full and final identification of the attraction of that first boyhood turn, and a definitive commitment to it. He had journeyed close enough to that new source of gravity to see its face and hear its name. The continuity and essential identity between the two

24. O, 33.

"turns" is the key to understanding Chesterton in his deepest and most personal thought.

We shall not go into the details of the Age of Decadence which forms the backdrop of his mental and moral crisis. Chesterton himself does not regard that ambience as causing, but only as fostering his confusion.

> Something may have been due to the atmosphere of the Decadents, and their perpetual hints of the luxurious horrors of paganism; but I am not disposed to dwell much on that defence; I suspect I manufactured most of the morbidities myself.[25]

Chesterton's escape from these morbidities, which I shall in a moment describe, forms the desperate itinerary of his pilgrimage. Followed out to its term, the young man achieved speculative and moral principles which he retained throughout his life. Indeed, one biographer wrote that "pages of his [schoolboy] notebooks could be woven into *Orthodoxy* [1908], essays from *The Debater* [likewise an adolescent production] introduced into *The Victorian Age in Literature* [1912], and it would simply look like buds and flowers on the same bush. In pure literature, philosophy and theology, he remains untouched by the faintest change."[26] Ronald Knox commented on how "his work burst upon the world with an astonishing maturity of observation and of thought."[27] The important thing to grasp is that this basic philosophy of life constituted the upshot of his adolescent pilgrimage. It was not the seasoned, "late" Chesterton who found it. He had kicked most of the mud off his shoes by the time he left school.

25. AB, 88–89.

26. Maisie Ward, *Gilbert Keith Chesterton* (New York: Sheed & Ward, 1943), 185.

27. Ronald Knox, "G.K. Chesterton: The Man and His Work," in *The Listener*, June 18, 1941, 8.

> As I was still thinking the thing out by myself, with little help from philosophy and no real help from religion, I invented a rudimentary theory of my own.[28]

The two discovered principles were so rich in potency that forty years of prolific writing in a dizzying display of versatility were but the lavish parturition of their energies. To identify this point of departure of the man's thought, we need to turn to but one chapter in his *Autobiography.* The story told in that chapter, candidly entitled "How to be a Lunatic," provides us with the only key that can unlock the logic of Chesterton's immense and manifold opus. Many other biographical details are interesting and in varying degrees bear upon his thought; this event alone generates his thought and lies forever at its source. It was his youthful trek to these simple lights that constitutes his brief and dramatic odyssey.

After Chesterton had finished secondary school at St. Paul's, instead of going on to college with his intellectual colleagues, he decided instead to pursue an artistic career and entered Slade Art School. It was here, from 1892 to 1895, that the young artist met with the two forces which were to galvanize his mind into an articulate and perpetual intellectual rebound.

One force was mental, and the other was moral. First, the mental:

> At a very early age I had thought my way back to thought itself. It is a very dreadful thing to do; for it may lead to thinking that there is nothing but thought. At this time I did not distinguish between dreaming and waking; not only as a mood, but as a metaphysical doubt, I felt as if everything might be a dream. It was as if I had myself projected the universe from within, with all its trees and stars; and that is manifestly even nearer to going mad.[29]

28. AB, 89.
29. Ibid., 88.

Then came the moral, or better, immoral force:

> And as with mental, so with moral extremes. There is something truly menacing in the thought of how quickly I could imagine the maddest, when I had never committed the mildest crime. . . . There was a time when I had reached that condition of moral anarchy within, in which a man says, in the words of Wilde, that "Atys with the blood-stained knife were better than the thing I am." [30]

This dual crisis bore upon 1) the theory about the world around him to which his mind had assented, and 2) the choice of laws he had made for the orientation of his behavior. The source of his morbid flirtations with solipsism and anarchy was a certain "unresolved riddle of the mind" that plagued him in that "period of life in which the mind is merely dreaming and drifting; and often drifting onto very dangerous rocks."[31]

He felt tempted, as any of us might, by "a very negative and even nihilistic philosophy. And though I never accepted it altogether, it threw a shadow over my mind and made me feel that *most profitable and worthy ideas were, as it were, on the defensive*."[32] [emphasis added] As an art student, the current rage over Impressionism served as an apt metaphor for his mental mushiness, for

> it naturally lends itself to the metaphysical suggestion that things only exist as we perceive them, or that things do not exist at all. The philosophy of Impressionism is necessarily close to the philosophy of illusion. And this atmosphere also tended to contribute, however indirectly, to a certain mood of unreality and sterile isolation that settled at this time upon me; and I think upon many others.[33]

30. Ibid., 88–89.
31. Ibid., 86.
32. Ibid., 86–87.
33. Ibid., 87.

Likewise, an early experience with one of his boyhood acquaintances sums up his encounter with the tempting allurements of evil. The text is long, but too big a help to curtail. Referring to a chat he had before his fireplace with this frightening young companion of his, he comments:

> It was strange, perhaps, that I liked his dirty, drunken society; it was stranger still, perhaps, that he liked my society. . . . And I shall never forget the half-hour in which he and I argued about real things for the first and last time. . . .
>
> He had a horrible fairness of the intellect that made me despair of his soul. A common, harmless atheist would have denied that religion produced humility or humility a simple joy; but he admitted both. He only said, "But shall I not find in evil a life of its own? Granted that for every woman I ruin one of these red sparks will go out; will not the expanding pleasure of ruin. . . ."
>
> "Do you see that fire?" I asked. "If we had a real fighting democracy, someone would burn you in it; like the devil-worshiper that you are."
>
> "Perhaps," he said, in his tired, fair way. "Only what you call evil I call good."
>
> He went down the great steps alone, and I felt as if I wanted the steps swept and cleaned. I followed later, and as I went to find my hat in the low passage where it hung, I suddenly heard his voice again, but the words were inaudible. I stopped, startled; but then I heard the voice of one of the vilest of his associates saying, "Nobody can possibly know." And then I heard those two or three words which I remember in every syllable and cannot forget. I heard the Diabolist say, "I tell you I have done everything else. If I do that I shan't know the difference between right and wrong." I rushed out without daring to pause; and as I passed the fire I did not know whether it was hell or the furious love of God.
>
> I have since heard that he died; it may be said, I think, that he committed suicide; though he did it with tools of

> pleasure, not with tools of pain. God help him, I know the road he went; but I have never known or even dared to think what was that place at which he stopped and refrained.[34]

Casting about for harbor on this impressionistic ocean of subjectivism with its tempting eddies of evil, the young Chesterton made his momentous discovery: it was not the world that was at fault, neither in its wild intransigence in the face of reason nor in the nameless temptations with which it abounds. No, the world was basically innocent. It was Chesterton who was at fault. Something in him was awry. And it did not take long to find out what was upsetting his mind's balance:

> The essential reason was that my eyes were turned inwards rather than outwards; giving my moral personality, I should imagine, a very unattractive squint. I was still oppressed with the metaphysical nightmare of negations about mind and matter, with the morbid images of evil, with the burden of my own mysterious brain and body; but by this time I was in revolt against them; and trying to construct a healthier conception of cosmic life. . . .[35]

His speculative doubt about the world and moral doubt about law turned out to be but the shadows of the two principles with which he is finally confronted.

After what seems to have been nearly three years of anguished darkness on these two matters, Chesterton emerged rather dramatically from the cloud with two indelible convictions etched in iron on the edge of his intellect:

1. The world is real and is our first teacher.
2. Sin is real and is our first tempter.

34. Ward, 45–46.
35. AB, 97–98.

Only when these two facts became explicitly evident to Chesterton's "congested imagination" could he begin to put together what he calls his "rudimentary and make-shift theory." Sifting these two principles out of all his words, and using for the task the sieve of the Aristotelian distinction between speculative and moral modes of knowledge, may seem at first an artificial device and untrue to the spontaneity of our author. The abundance of texts, however, which obey this scheme in no uncertain terms, should be enough to belie the suspicion. We will be returning to these two themes throughout the book, and attempting to exhibit the harmonic and ever varying counterpoint they play to all the issues Chesterton discusses.

That our author arrives at these principles as a young man, and merely elucidates and expands upon them as he grows, bears witness to his "thesis that there is something real behind all these first movements of the mind."[36] In an almost Platonic *anamnesis*, he links up these two truths with the mind of the child, to which the unmoored adult mind must finally return if it is to find port again. The truths are not fresh achievements. They are recovered realizations, for it was in childhood that they were born.

> I was subconsciously certain then, as I am consciously certain now, that there [i.e., in childhood] was the white and solid road and the worthy beginning of the life of man; and that it is man who afterwards darkens it with dreams or goes astray from it in self-deception. It is only the grown man who lives a life of make-believe and pretending; and it is he who has his head in a cloud.[37]

When Chesterton finally got his boyish head out of the cloud and returned to the solid earth of his childhood, he saw and he remembered:

36. Ibid., 106.
37. Ibid., 49.

> Mere existence, reduced to its most primary limits, was extraordinary enough to be exciting. Anything was magnificent as compared with nothing. . . . At the back of our brains, so to speak, there was a forgotten blaze or burst of astonishment at our own existence. The object of the artistic and spiritual life was to dig for this submerged sunrise of wonder.[38]

Looking back still later, he wrote:

> I had in childhood, and have partly preserved out of childhood, a certain romance of receptiveness, which has not been killed by sin or even by sorrow; for though I have not had great troubles, I have had many. A man does not grow old without being bothered; but I have grown old without being bored. Existence is still a strange thing to me; and as a stranger I give it welcome.[39]

Reflecting further on the concomitant moral dilemma, he observes:

> This is the same period of youth which is full of doubts, of morbidities and temptations; and which, though in my case mainly subjective, has left in my mind for ever a certitude upon the objective solidity of sin.[40]

And though temptation was present, the real maker of his sins was no other than himself:

> I was already quite certain that I could if I chose cut myself off from the whole life of the universe. Though I was more foggy about ethical and theological matters than I am now, I was quite clear on that issue; that there was a final adversary, and that you might find a man resolutely turned away from goodness.[41]

38. Ibid., 90.
39. Ibid., 352–53.
40. Ibid., 75.
41. Ibid., 77.

It is the singular conjunction of Chesterton's theoretical crisis with his moral crisis which is most instructive. The thought of pure intellectual independence, of complete originality of concept, of mothering forth a world out of one's own lonely brain—this seemingly innocuous experiment of idle speculation brought in its train an imaginative zoo of hideous temptations and demonic enormities. Fortunately, however, it worked conversely with his new, make-shift theory. That is to say, while digging for that submerged sunrise of wonder, he not only regained the principles of all healthy human cogitation, but he also discovered the bedrock of all morality and the thrill of true liberty: the liberty that is free to bind itself to the good. We will see how the initial speculative doubt about the first data of the senses sets the stage for a first moral doubt about the natural target of the will.

It was stated in the last chapter that Chesterton's achievement of these two evidences, or his return to these two principles, is characterized by him as a "homecoming." And yet it is a home from which he had become culpably alienated. Perhaps his favorite plot was that of the man, who, one fine day, set out from his own home in search of his own home. In 1912 appeared the full-length novel about the adventures of such a seeker, *Manalive*. But already in the 1890's his little story "Homesick at Home" told the tale of White Wynd:

> "That green cornfield through the window," he said dreamily, "shining in the sun. Somehow, somehow it reminds me of a field outside my own home."
>
> "Your own home?" cried his wife. "This is your home!"
>
> White Wynd rose to his feet, seeming to fill the room. He stretched forth his hand and took a staff. He stretched it forth again and took a hat. The dust came in clouds from both of them.
>
> "Father," cried one child, "where are you going?"
>
> "Home," he replied.
>
> "What can you mean? *This* is your home. What home are you going to?"

"To the White Farmhouse by the river."

"This is it!"

He was looking at them very tranquilly when his eldest daughter caught sight of his face.

"Oh, he is mad!" she screamed, and buried her face in her hands.

He spoke calmly. "You are a little like my eldest daughter."[42]

There is something that keeps us from home. Indeed, there is something that keeps home from us. And that something is, to return to the beginning of this book, a lassitude in our faculty of appreciation. White Wynd travels the world to return to his home because "his heart had grown stale and bitter towards the wife and children whom he saw every day. . . . Prose had got hold of him: the sealing of the eyes and the closing of the ears."[43]

Recurrently, Chesterton insists upon the surprising makeup of the world, which presents itself to the mind of man as a quite "strange world," one that could have been quite different from how it in fact is, or which could very well have never come about at all. He finds telltale signs of freely chosen acts and unplumbed purposes. The world matters, and its saner citizens yearn to know why. Any attempt to obviate the two evidences that lead to all these instincts, or to deny their evidence by attempting to grind them out with the machinery of syllogisms, does something to the mind. It freezes it. Halted in its flight by this sudden stop, the mind drops like a stone onto the foreign terrain we mentioned before. Thought stops, and something else, something uncanny, begins. Chesterton spent enough time looking about, panic-stricken, upon the pessimistic, solipsistic world

42. "Daylight and Nightmare," in *Uncollected Stories and Essays*, selected by Marie Smith (London: Xanadu, 1986), 24.

43. Ibid., 23.

his mind was making, to feel confident enough to make a claim. After he had emerged, galvanized into a fortified insistence on his two principles, he announced to all who cared to read his books that he had tracked down the designs of that double doubt to its secret lair.

In his first volume of Father Brown detective stories, several years later, Chesterton speaks through the character of the detective-priest who, in one of the stories, had just spoken with an Indian brahman. What we shall later analyze philosophically, these words of Fr. Brown give us in a glance:

> "When that Indian spoke to us," went on Brown in a conversational undertone, "I had a sort of vision, a vision of him and all his universe. Yet he only said the same thing three times. When first he said, 'I want nothing,' it meant only that he was impenetrable, that Asia does not give itself away. Then he said again, 'I want nothing,' and I knew that he meant that he was sufficient to himself, like a cosmos, that he needed no God, neither admitted any sins. And when he said the third time, 'I want nothing,' he said it with blazing eyes. And I knew that he meant literally what he said; that nothing was his desire and his home; that he was weary for nothing as for wine; that annihilation, the mere destruction of everything or anything. . . ."[44]

Long puzzled by the provenance of his youthful temptations and obscurities, Chesterton believed he had found their breeding ground at last. In a still later work, this time an essay, Chesterton spoke again of

> that turn or twist towards Oriental fancies and the paradox of pessimism, which always comes to Europeans as something fresh when their own sanity seems to be something stale . . . these appalling ideas, that a man has no individual destiny, that making a minute item in the tribe or hive, is his only earthly destiny, these ideas do come all together

44. "The Wrong Shape," in *The Innocence of Fr. Brown.*

> out of the same quarter; they do in practice blow upon us out of the East, as cold and inhuman as the east wind.[45]

G.K. Chesterton's pilgrimage as a young man turns out to be, on close examination, a retreat from a deterministic pessimism denying liberty, a monistic pantheism denying creation, and an etherealized mysticism denying personality, all generating huge practical anomalies in the social sphere in the understanding and protection of the state, the family, and private property. All of these menaces betray the characteristic marks of that bent of mind Westerners usually term "Oriental." Now what I think it is essential to see is that *these philosophical and social aberrations were diagnosed by Chesterton as the ultimate progeny of the initial violation of the first evidences of the mind.*

And that violation turns out to be oddly common to the Eastern thought most typically peddled in the West—at least in Chesterton's day—and (*notate bene!*) the most characteristic philosophies of modern European thought. To this last we shall soon return. That he had been vexed by them in late 19th-century Europe was only evidence that these peculiarly "Eastern" heresies had broken in freshly, though certainly not for the first time, upon the West.

> Asia stands for something which the world in the West as well as the East is more and more feeling as a presence, and even a pressure. It might be called the spiritual world let loose; or a sort of psychical anarchy; a jungle of mango plants. And it is pressing upon the West also today because of the breaking down of certain materialistic barriers that have hitherto held it back.[46]

Only since the early 19th century did Europe begin to have access to initial, though imperfect, translations of some of

45. WB, 201–2.
46. NJ, 156.

the classic Hindu and Buddhist texts and their reflections on reality. Their apparent accord with much of German Idealism, for instance, was an omen often remarked upon by Chesterton.

> For this [Occidental] world of different and varied beings is especially the world of the Christian Creator, the world of created things, like things made by an artist; as compared with the world that is only one thing, with a sort of shimmering and shifting veil of misleading change; which is the conception of so many of the ancient religions of Asia and the modern sophistries of Germany.[47]

We earlier underscored one phrase out of the *Autobiography* where the author remarked on how he had discovered that "most profitable and worthy ideas were, as it were, on the defensive." For him these "profitable and worthy ideas" so in need of defense were ideas that have, for various reasons, developed only in the West. And it is they that have intellectually nourished all that is best in what we know as Western civilization. But, curiously, they seem to be forever under threat. And the main mental trouble with modern Europe is identified by Chesterton as a particularly wholesale abandonment of those precious sanities. Our trouble is that we have surrendered to and are increasingly being absorbed by certain fundamental Oriental errors in thought; or, to be more precise, errors in the beginnings of thought.

This polarization of West and East, and the equation of much modern Western thought with perennial Eastern thought, will seem facile to some. But Chesterton himself was careful to avoid a mere black-and-white discrimination.

> Now this scheme of east and west is inadequate; but it does happen to fit in with the working facts. For the odd thing is this, not only are most of the merely modern move-

47. TA, 223–24.

ments of idealism Oriental, but their Orientalism is all that they have in common. They all come together, and yet their only apparent point of union is that they all come from the East.[48]

In this passage, our author is referring to enthusiasts of teetotalism and vegetarianism, among others. But even these "ideals" bear the signature of deeper "ideas":

It is ideas that have come to us out of the depths of Asia; and especially all the wrong ideas. I know, of course, that *there are many other ideas in so vast and complex a continent; and many that are by no means so wrong.* But I am talking, not of the ideas that are deepest in Asia, of which I necessarily know little; but of the Asiatic ideals that have bitten deepest into Europe, of which I know only too much.[49] [emphasis added]

As we shall see later, the modern world has been in many ways initiated into these Eastern ideas, although their ultimate provenance, according to Chesterton, is beyond the geographical "East."

I do not accept this dull definition of locality; It is a spirit in Asia, and even a spirit that can be named. It is approximately described as an insane simplicity. In all these cases we find people attempting to perfect a thing solely by simplification; by obliterating special features: this cosmos is full of wingless birds, of hornless cattle, of hairless women, and colorless wine, all fading into a formless background.[50]

[It is] the philosophy ultimately represented by the snake devouring its tail; the awful skeptical argument in a circle by which everything begins and ends in the mind. I would far rather be a fetish worshiper and have a little fun, than be an oriental pessimist expected always to smile like an opti-

48. WB, 201.
49. GS, 26.
50. WB, 202.

> mist. Now it seems to me that the fighting Christian creed is the one thing that has been in that mystical circle and broken out of it, and become something real as well. It has gone westward by a sort of centrifugal force, like a stone from a sling. . . .[51]

Surveying the dozens of volumes of Gilbert Chesterton's writings, a kind of underlying intellectual crusade can be discerned; and like the original Crusades, it too is also a pilgrimage. One can even say that Chesterton's crusade is literally in the service of the Cross, but not only in its historic sense of the Rood of Christ, but also in its symbolic sense as the sign which marks the boundaries between heaven and earth, between God and creature, between person and person. The richest treasures of our Western tradition are all predicated on the existence of those boundaries, and some of the recurring attractions of the East on their negation. Good fences make good neighbors. The good fence of Western philosophy can make a neighbor even of a Hindu; but the fence will be built with Western wood, and men like Chesterton will have chopped down the trees.

3. THE RHETORICIAN

The pilgrimage of Chesterton's philosophic mind from what he understood to be the borderless cogitations of the East to the clear, created edges of the West, was already complete by the time he wrote *Orthodoxy* in 1908. He would certainly have stressed, looking back at all this later in life, that the pilgrimage was only consummated with his Catholic baptism in 1922. But, as I have maintained, that event merely sealed with a final act of the will what had already been intellectually apprehended years before. His vision of life did not

51. NJ, 303.

really evolve, but only matured and resolved itself as he grew older. It merely spread itself out in a series of applications and an array of inferences.

Looking over the small library of books he penned, a new question now urges itself. We have already seen the capital quality in those books to be their philosophic content, and we have identified the pilgrim nature of its course and inspiration. The question of our author's choice of media is now before us. Why was it, from *Orthodoxy* to the *Autobiography*, that Chesterton wrote in so many genres, and especially that he held most doggedly to the resources of journalism?

This question we have already answered in part. Modern man's separation from the traditional cultural milieu of Western Christendom has necessitated that writers intent on restoring perennial philosophy offer that wisdom somehow re-housed in its largely lost ambience. Now we must ask if Chesterton's choice of journalism and his disaffection from academia did not somehow meet this need.

Chesterton's standard biographer uttered the frequently repeated regret that the man spent so many exhausting years in the grind of the journalist's profession—indeed, for the last 10 years as editor of his own weekly—when he could have been spending all those busy hours leisurely producing additional tomes like *The Everlasting Man* and *Orthodoxy.*

To be sure, the former book (according to most, his best) was possible only because he had a nearly two-year respite from the toils of editorship. Twenty such years might have given us any number of masterpieces of comparable stature. Instead, our journalist spread his words over thousands of articles, essays, prefaces to other authors' books, detective stories and the like. He seemed almost to relish hiding his gems, like parents hiding Easter eggs. The few longer works he did manage to get out in these years, such as *St. Francis of Assisi* and *St. Thomas Aquinas*, tantalize us still further. The remaining harvest is still rich, as we labor our way through mountains of yellowed newspapers, scissoring out little columns of Chestertonia; but the crazy-quilt summa we piece together out of such findings is of uneven quality, and lacks the mental orchestration of which our author is clearly capable.

But since these other books were never written, must we see Chesterton's years of editorship and article-writing as a sad loss—or at least as a substantial subtraction from what a more prudently managed genius would have offered us?

I think not. Certainly we must not make the error (one abhorrent to Chesterton) of seeing those years as "meant to be," as if his writing in newspapers was somehow written in the stars. This is nonsense. He could have followed the advice given him by family and friends and allowed his deceased brother's newspaper—which he had begun editing, in part as an homage to Cecil, who died in the Great War—to be buried along with him. However, it is too simple a solution to see his continuation of the paper as a mere tribute to the departed. Chesterton was aware that he had a mission, and it is inconceivable that he would have taken over the editorship of any paper if he could not see it as somehow serving that mission. Indeed, with whom had he shared that mission more than with Cecil?

Now, as it turns out, the two characteristics we have detected in his work as a whole do indeed invite the peculiar liberties and limitations of a journalist's typewriter. They suggest that our author's choice may have served his mission well. Chesterton's philosophical bent caused him to have something to say about nearly everything. He had a mind forever at boiling point, it seemed. A regular, disciplined organ of some sort, ready to record even the most casual and incidental utterances, would capture and perhaps even elicit much otherwise fugitive wisdom.

What better profession than the Fourth Estate? The stimulus of weekly deadlines kept his rich mind constantly on tap.

Whether it imprudently overtaxed his rich body is, of course, another question which we will leave to his biographers. In any case, it did not completely frustrate the development of longer trains of thought, as a series of articles could easily be gathered later into book form (as, for instance, *The Outline of Sanity*, composed of articles from *G.K.'s Weekly*).

A second advantage of this medium for Chesterton's mission was its audience. Throughout his life, his greatest concern was not for the academics and professionals, but instead for the "common man," the man in the street. This is the kind of man who is more likely to read inexpensive newspapers than costly books. But here a precision is needed. The common man Chesterton so loved was not just the "class" of everyday people, or the commonalty as opposed to an upper class. It would be more accurate to designate the target of his writing as that which is common to all men, that is, the element in everybody which is universal, that "certain thing that loves babies, that fears death, that likes sunlight."[52] That element is just more visible and more conscious of its power in the man in the street than in the agitated cerebra of the universities.

These two features in Chesterton's chosen career: 1) being able to address any topic, and 2) being free to use any literary form that might best communicate what he had to say to the common man—including fiction, poetry, essay, biography, current-events commentary, etc.—bring to mind the description given by Aristotle of a certain kind of discourse:

> Rhetoric is the counterpart of dialectic. Both alike are concerned with such things as come, more or less, within the general ken of all men and belong to no definite science.... Rhetoric may be defined as the faculty of observing in any given case the available means of persuasion on almost any subject presented to us; and that is why

52. CD, 109.

we say that, in its technical character, it is not concerned with any special or definite class of subjects.[53]

Chesterton was a rhetorician. Rhetoric for Aristotle and the classical tradition was identified normally with the mode of discourse proper to the political arena. And of course abuses in this arena can give the word "rhetoric" a ring of hollowness and sham. But the affinity of rhetoric and politics is not formal and absolute. It merely results from the contingent and intractable nature of the subject matter of politics, with its insubordination to strict scientific treatment. Rhetoric presents its various topics under the overriding criterion of persuasion—argumentative content being but one of three factors therein (the other two being the emotions of the audience and the character of the speaker). It is the only mode of discourse that can accommodate the circumstance-laden issues of the political order. But politics is not, as such, the proper subject matter of rhetoric. As Aristotle asserts, it has no proper subject matter.

The highest work of the rhetorician is to put the already-discovered truth, on whatever topic, in the best light possible, to assist that truth to prevail and to make it effective in the lives of his hearers. Cardinal Newman wrote that Aristotle "makes the very essence of the art to lie in the precise recognition of a hearer. It is a relative art, and in that respect differs from logic, which simply teaches the right use of reason, whereas rhetoric is the art of persuasion, which implies a person who is to be persuaded."[54] Chesterton excelled in this. And the particular affinity of his art to the political life was by no means lost on him. Concerned as he was with the fate of the men and women for whom he wrote, his most

53. Aristotle, *Rhetoric*, 1354a 1–3; 1355b 26.33–35 in R. McKeon, *Basic Works of Aristotle* (New York: Random House, 1971), 1325, 1329.

54. John Henry Cardinal Newman, *The Idea of a University* (New York: Image Books, 1959), 379.

adamant insistence on the importance of the speculative order issued with a torrent of dedication onto the practical field of social, political, and economic questions.

The rhetorician, therefore, has his eye always on the hearer, and is concerned primarily that he communicates his material, turning therefore to whatever means lend themselves best. Now clearly, Chesterton does not always succeed. Many a "common man" will at times find his writing quite over his head. But when he does succeed, it is as a rhetorician that he succeeds. He makes the truth effective. He brings it across to you, often with a smile. And he writes as a journalist because he finds in that medium the best contemporary forum for a teacher of men.

Chesterton never wrote a scientific book. He foreswore the use of footnotes, preferring to see his pages of prose stand on their own two feet. And he definitely was not what we would call a professional philosopher, but he may have been something better. He had more of what the first Greek philosophers attributed to obscure figures of old. Long before Plato wrote down his dialogues, or Aristotle his treatises, wise men taught much but wrote little or nothing. Instead, they left a trail of pregnant aphorisms wherever they went. If our author was not a philosopher, then it was not because he did not make the grade, but because he was closer to wisdom than even a philosopher is. Marshall McLuhan said of him that he possessed a "connaturality with every kind of reasonableness."[55] This is what one might better call a sage.

Of course, he did write. His writing is not systematic, but I hope to make clear by the end of this book that his thinking most certainly was. Those, however, who want his thought in systematic writing, need only turn to the great representatives of the Western perennial philosophy: Plato,

55. See Appendix, ref. 14.

Aristotle, Augustine and Aquinas, for starters. There you will find your dialogues, treatises, and summas spread out before you like a land of dreams. All of that got absorbed, at least in its guiding principles, into the great mountain of man called Chesterton. But the great man shakes his shaggy head and refuses to give it back to you as a map. Instead, he will take you by the hand and walk through the landscape with you—one lesson at a time. He keeps you laughing so much, you hardly notice that you are taking what really amounts to a remedial course in Western sanity. To characterize this special gift of rhetorical pedagogy, we might apply to Chesterton the following words Cicero wrote on the good orator:

> A good speaker is one who could speak with adequate acuteness and perspicacity before an ordinary audience from the point of view of what may be called the average intelligence, but a real orator is one who could add a charm and glamour of magnificence to the theme of his choice, and hold within the compass of his own mind and memory all the springs of knowledge on all subjects which had any bearing on oratory.[56]

It is the common man who must live with the commonest things, such as being and life and liberty and all the appurtenances of a universe. To address the commonest of men about the grandest of topics was the rhetorical aspiration of Chesterton. After all, he once said, "if the ordinary man may not discuss existence, why should he be asked to conduct it?" His seeming "connaturality with every kind of reasonableness" made his language approach that Scriptural quality identified by another great rhetorician, St. Augustine:

> [T]he words with which they are said seem not to have been sought by the speaker but to have been joined to the things spoken about as if spontaneously, like wisdom com-

56. Cicero, "On the Character of the Orator," nr. 21, in *Basic Works of Cicero* (New York: Modern Library, 1951), 201.

ing from her house. . . . Therefore, a certain eloquent man said, and said truly, that he who is eloquent should speak in such a way that he teaches, delights, and moves. Then he added, 'To teach is a necessity, to please is a sweetness, to persuade is a victory.'[57]

Chesterton's "metaphysical rhetoric" is perhaps best characterized as a philosophic tonic for reconditioning the mind and sensibility of modern man back into conformity with the common-sense evidences of saner times. We shall see how this meant for Chesterton, and means for us even more today, a "Journey to the *West*"—a return to three embattled but still sovereign corner-stones of common sense: the delight and liberty of an active but realistic imagination, the situation of personality and love at the very heart of being, and the discovery that the reign of reason can only be defended within a world of wonder.

57. St. Augustine, *On Christian Doctrine*, IV, 6.12 (New York: Library of Liberal Arts, 1958), 124, 136.

II

The Great Refusal of Modern Philosophy

"Afraid!" cried Gale, as if with indignation; "afraid you are a materialist! You haven't got much notion of what there really is to be afraid of! Materialists are all right; they are at least near enough to heaven to accept the earth and not imagine they made it. The dreadful doubts are not the doubts of the materialist. The dreadful doubts, the deadly and damnable doubts, are the doubts of the idealist."

~ G.K.C., *The Poet and the Lunatics*[1]

1. THE TURN OF A STRANGE CENTURY

As Chesterton stepped forth out of the cloud of his intellectual and moral trial, he found himself standing at the uneasy threshold of the 20th century. That century was to bring to fruition most of the brave new innovations the modern world had sired. Already in the first year, several of these novelties were sowing their own seeds. With no attempt to follow an exhaustive historical analysis, I shall highlight the cases which touch most upon our subject, contrast them with the aspirations of three major modern philosophers,

1. PL, 124.

and then review a few of the revealing cultural coordinates behind them.

In the year 1900 Chesterton published his first book.[2] That same year saw the appearance of Sigmund Freud's first major work, *On the Interpretation of Dreams*, opening to public view the strange and troubling world of the unconscious. Also in that year, Edmund Husserl's *Logical Investigations* was published, which, in suggestive counterpoint to Freud's book, began the pursuit of a similarly amorphous "pure consciousness." (We shall have occasion to return to this.) Later in the same year, the physicist Max Planck made the surprising discovery that energy seems to exist in discrete quanta, thus laying the foundation of quantum mechanics, and much of our 20th-century preoccupation with the atom. In a related development, Albert Einstein was busy elaborating his Special Theory of Relativity, and with it, the famous formula $E = mc^2$, destined to become the deceptively simple recipe for the conversion of cosmos back into chaos.

In the political and economic sphere, the immense British Empire, geographically the largest the world has known, attained its summit during the Boer War (1899–1902). At that summit, however, the corruption of an all-too-acquisitive appetite in much of modern capitalism showed its true colors. Almost antiphonally, at the other end of Europe, in January of 1900, Vladimir Lenin emerged from political exile in Siberia. He was soon to publish his book *What Is to Be Done?*, outlining his "party-system" construal of Marxist communism, and the program that was to engineer the civil society of one-third of the coming century's population.

In a brief purview of the arts at this juncture, we notice that Arnold Schönberg had just written his string sextet,

2. *Greybeards at Play*, a book of comic verse, followed by another book of poems, *The Wild Knight and Other Poems*; in 1901, his first book of essays appeared: *The Defendant*.

"The Transfigured Night," straining the seams of traditional tonality, and carrying Richard Wagner's chromatic liberties to such an extreme, the stirrings of an imminent break with tonality could already be sensed. Likewise, Gustav Mahler was filling the last decade of the 19th century and the first of the 20th with a kind of final apotheosis of the post-Romantic effort at grandiose expression: huge, sprawling symphonies, similarly loosened from the strict discipline of standard tonality. The new age seemed to be rehearsing a new tune—but with less tone. In painting, the last mists of Impressionism were evaporating, and a young generation of upcoming Fauvists and Cubists looked to Africa and primitive man for their models. Soon the dislocated faces of Picasso, and a chaos of disjointed visual impressions, would hold themselves up to the new century like a cruelly candid mirror.

A further indication of this new preoccupation with the primitive was the appearance of James Frazer's *Golden Bough* on just about every academic's desk, with a 12-volume expansion in preparation. In this work, the eyes of Europe were directed towards the primitive "magical" and "religious" cultures of the world, from which our so fortunate "scientific" culture had allegedly evolved. In these same years, Ernst Haeckel, the German biologist, was busy drawing genealogical trees of animal evolution, urging modern man to face the music and assume his spot on one of the branches. His influential *Riddles of the Universe* appeared also in 1900, offering a monistic-pantheistic interpretation of Darwinism to which many pace-setting intellectuals turned in admiration.

One could effortlessly add to this list, but let this suffice. I wish to remark only upon one characteristic of all these new movements that shape the world in which Chesterton came of age. They all strangely focus on rather isolated and featureless details of our physical or psychic world: electromagnetic quanta, minuscule alterations in millions of years of biological evolution, the twelve bland semi-tones of the octave in music, the *tohuwabohu* of the unconscious, the material conditions of the "historic process," and a host of others—all to the increasing exclusion of the proportioned, human point of view. And that point of view is the total one, the habitual one, capable of taking in the whole, however unresolved that whole might still be. It is this orthodox, philosophic standpoint which Chesterton will especially attempt to rescue. Early on in the century, he wrote:

> [T]he modern world is full of a phenomenon peculiar to itself—I mean the spectacle of small or originally small things swollen to enormous size and power. The modern world is like a world in which toadstools should be as big as trees, and insects should walk about in the sun as large as elephants. Thus, for instance, the shopkeeper, almost an unimportant figure in carefully ordered states, has in our time become the millionaire, and has more power than ten kings.... In short, our age is a sort of splendid jungle in which some of the most towering weeds and blossoms have come from the smallest seed.[3]
>
> The characteristic of modern movements *par excellence* is the apotheosis of the insignificant.[4]

Not that all of these new theories are without value. Chesterton will write in *Orthodoxy* that the trouble with the modern world lies not so much in its vices, as in its virtues gone wild. One might extrapolate upon this observation and maintain that another trouble with the modern world is not so much its falsehoods, as its truths gone wild—not even new truths, but rather old truths in new isolation.

> [W]hat is new is not the idea, but only the isolation of the idea... the absurd fancy that these modern philosophies are modern in the sense that the great men of the past did

3. ACD, 115–16.
4. RB, 165.

> not think of them. They thought of them; only they did not think much of them.[5]

All these newly sequestered ideas were slowly eating away at both the common securities of reason and the supernatural assurances of Christianity. Words Chesterton penned later in this new century could well stand over its first half as epigraph, if not epitaph:

> The most curious feature of the time is the continuous soft collapse of one thing after another, like sand castles sapped by the sea; of almost everything except (as I should say) of one tradition of truth that is not of this earth, and certain hard facts that are very specially of this earth.[6]

It is indeed this *earth* that modern man has somehow lost. He is accused, of course, of materialism, but even his grip on matter has grown limp. He has been taught to fix his bewildered imagination on the billions of atoms he sits upon and learn to forget the chair; to "see" the stars racing away from us and one another at enormous velocities, and forget the vault of the starry sky; to look with pathetic obsession upon man's coccyx and ear muscles (two supposed vestiges of our evolutionary past, back when we could wag our tails and wiggle our ears at mealtimes), with a clear imaginary picture of a graduated parade of anthropoids evolving their way up millions of years—up to the accidental node of genetic arithmetic called "man." All the while he fails to see the most imaginative part of all: the image of God. This fragmentation of man's imagination before a flurry of deracinated truths and half-truths is the saddest plight of the 20th century. Rediscovering the lost integer is the task our author set for himself.

Chesterton's celebration of the peasant will never be

5. CM, 23–24.
6. FA, 178.

understood to be anything more than a ridiculous romantic affectation unless one thing is grasped. For Chesterton, the peasant is not important because he is poor, but because he is whole.

> The peasant does live, not merely a simple life, but a complete life. It may be very simple in its completeness. The community is at present very defective because there is not in the core of it any such simple consciousness.[7]

All of our author's vast literary, philosophical and apologetic production impinges very early upon the greatest social questions of his day. Other comparable Christian writers of modern, industrial society, such as John Henry Newman and C.S. Lewis, exhibit a genius more trained upon the spiritual or literary spheres. Chesterton's mind, in contrast, races into the heart of all the political and economic altercations of his day, and a fat stack of books and pamphlets testify to his dedication. But this must be looked at not only on the surface of its evident Christian charity and broad human appreciation, but also in its less evident, but more ultimate roots. Chesterton was a thinker, and his leap into the social arena would not have been so vigorous were it not in some profound way nourished by that thought. His defense of the peasant was, in fine, a function of his defense of sane philosophy.

The peasant simply represents the common core of sane humanity, still attached quite physically to the earth, and thus exhibits the most embracing human appreciation of the world and its variety of subordinate causes. The peasant's cracker-barrel philosophy represents the common sense of mankind. In saner times, the peasant preserved it, and only someone like him will be able to do so in the future.

> What is wrong with the man in the modern town is that he does not know the causes of things; and that is why, as the

7. OS, 130–31.

> poet says, he can be too much dominated by despots and demagogues. He does not know where things come from; he is the type of cultivated Cockney who said he liked milk out of a clean shop and not a dirty cow. The more elaborate is the town organization, the more elaborate even is the town education, the less is he the happy man of Virgil who knows the causes of things.[8]
>
> [In saner times] there would be somewhere in the centre of civilization a type that was truly independent; the sense of producing and consuming within its own social circle. I do not say that such a complete human life stands for a complete humanity. I do not say that the State needs only the man who needs nothing from the State. But I do say that this man who supplies his own needs is very much needed. I say it is largely because of his absence from modern civilization, that modern civilization has lost unity. It is nobody's business to note the whole process, to see where things come from and where they go to. Nobody follows the whole winding river of milk as it flows from the cow to the baby.... We need a social circle in which things constantly return to those that threw them; and men who know the end and the beginning and the rounding of our little life.[9]

In the modern, industrialized West, the man on the land no longer sets the tone of human sensibility, and the urbanized mind looks predominantly upon a world made by man, and thus understandable by man. The very confusions of this wild technology have sent him on strange odysseys in search of meaning: down into the unconscious, backwards through the fuzzy lines of evolution, upward into the galaxies, and anywhere whence a new pedagogue seems to be hailing. But the one great pedagogue into whose face we daily gaze—I mean the world *itself*, encountered in unaided sense

8. Ibid., 133.
9. Ibid., 136–37.

experience—on him we turn our backs, and sooner or later break them, for flunking this primary school means never getting past lesson one in anything.

This great refusal began in the 17th century. The new philosophers' chief complaint about our first look at the world as pedagogue was that it seemed so notoriously imprecise and illogical. Accordingly, they endeavored to find a newer, better, and more mathematical tutor within a new perspective, thus cleaning up the business of thought once and for all. The irony of all this is that it was precisely this newly launched pilgrimage toward precision that has landed us, three centuries thence, in the misty caverns of all these disorienting 20th-century queries. Chesterton saw this, and his book *Orthodoxy*, which we shall closely examine in the following part of this book, is an attempt to restore us to the tutelage of God's universe. But before we approach that restoration, we need to look back upon the fascinating story of how man first came to refuse the ministrations of the first salute of the universe.

2. PALIMPSESTS OF PRINCIPLES

"Have you ever seen a fellow fail at the high jump because he had not gone far enough back for his run? That is Modern Thought. It is so confident of where it is going to that it does not know where it comes from."[10] I hope to show that it is precisely by its confidence that it can *go to* first principles that much modern philosophy no longer *comes from* them.

We who are investigating first principles have already been thinking for many years and will find it impossible to recapture those inaugural cerebrations first performed in our mother's arms. Modern philosophy, however, has been fret-

10. UD, 83.

ting over this question for the better part of 400 years. From the 17th century to the 20th, the quest has been underway of some virginal, unmapped island of pure thought, from the shores of which the ship of philosophy could be freshly launched. On this celebrated maiden voyage, many goals were set which were philosophically to match the geographical glories of Christopher Columbus and John Cabot. The sea thereby charted, it was hoped, would be deep and clear and quickly sounded with greatest precision.

Ever since these new odysseys began, cries of discovery have periodically rung out over the continent. But only three have gained a sizable following. One can almost give them a century apiece, as a kind of territorial claim. Their names are well known, though the latter is still better known through his followers. The first was René Descartes, who inspired most late 17th- and, by implication, nearly all 18th-century philosophy. The second was Immanuel Kant, to whom the 19th century looked as to a philosophical Moses. The third was Edmund Husserl, who so brilliantly revamped the Cartesian platform that some of the most influential 20th-century thinkers (such as Heidegger and Sartre) have taken their cues from him. Each of these gifted thinkers agreed that modern man needs to start thinking all over again, and offered his own program to the purpose. Their times and temperaments were different, but each offered, *ceteris paribus,* a three-fold program of like inspiration, containing 1) a regime of intellectual purgation to rid the mind of accumulated error and habits of imprecision and distortion; 2) a newly isolated and carefully outlined principle with which to reignite the engines of the overhauled mind; and 3) an exact and painstaking new method of procedure for conducting philosophy in a rigorously "scientific" manner.

There is obviously a world of issues and controversies involved in the philosophies of these three masters. None, however, is as pivotal as the one to which we shall limit ourselves here, namely, the very way in which each of them proposed to "start thinking all over again." They made no bones about it. Each was quite programmatic in proposing his newly forged purges, principles and methods as long-needed antidotes to a certain fault in thought which had allegedly blurred the philosophical enterprise before their day.

The words of Francis Bacon were still ringing in their ears: "There remains but one course for the recovery of a sound and healthy condition; namely, that the entire work of the understanding be commenced afresh, and the mind itself be from the very outset not left to take its own course, but guided at every step; and the business be done as if by machinery."[11] To be sure, each of them had several ancient evils to combat, but there was one which, in their judgment, had especially befuddled and misdirected the Western philosophical mind. And it was this: the endemic human habit of taking the first salute of the universe at face value. Chesterton's pilgrimage was aimed at a recovery of this beleaguered protocol. He himself had lost his hold on it through the suggestive offerings of modern thought and culture. And when he finally regained it, it was in deliberate rebellion against these offerings. It is for this reason that we must dwell on the origin and gestation of their philosophical articulation.

None of our three modern revolutionaries made so bold as to suggest that he was the first ever to propose such a skeptical squint at the world's first greeting. Plato, and the tradition he unwittingly sired, had long ago filled many Western thinkers with a sense of distrust before the fickle moods and multiple deceptions of sense experience. Reflections on this had led many to posit a transcendent world of one sort or another, and to have it serve as the real target of

11. Francis Bacon, *Magna Instauratio*, Preface, in *Essays, Advancement of Learning, New Atlantis and Other Pieces*, ed. R.F. Jones (New York, 1937), 268.

our mind's quest for enduring truth. But though a world beyond was pursued, the world here below—as fragile as it may appear—was never really doubted. Its first salute may have been indistinct, but it was always taken to be un-doubtable, indeed, redoubtable. In short, in ancient and medieval philosophy, there never really existed what we have come to call "the problem of the external world," or "the critical problem." Serious discussions were held on whether or not God or the gods exist, on whether or not *we* will exist beyond the grave, or on how long the world has existed, or will exist. But no one seemed to have ever put the question as to whether or not the world *now* exists. Those who may have done so were nicely silenced, or ignored, for no record of their voices survives.

The centuries passed, human experience accumulated, and the "adult reading and art" of the Renaissance and the "grown-up religion" of the Reformation caused many to wonder if it were not high time for philosophy to shake off its protracted pubescence. It seemed foreordained that this enlightened coming-of-age would naturally pass on from letters, the arts and religion to philosophy too. Kant was to give it a classic formulation in his famous definition of *Aufklärung* (enlightenment):

> Enlightenment is the freeing of man from his self-imposed state of minority, which is the inability to use one's understanding without the guidance of another. This state of minority comes about when its source lies not in the lack of understanding, but rather in the lack of the determination and courage to use it without the help of another.[12]

We shall see that for philosophy intellectual *majority* came to mean precisely that one had come to accept the "critical problem" as the only serious and effective initiation of the

12. Immanuel Kant, *Was ist Aufklärung?* (Berlinische Monatsschrift: 1784) [my translation].

mind into the pursuit of wisdom. But what is crucial to us here is not whether or not there is something beyond the experienced world, to which the mind can eventually turn. The issue is, rather, whether one accepts *this* world's first self-introduction as reliable, "on the level," "sincere," as it were, or sees it instead as duplicitous, pretending to be what it is not, and involving those who take it at face value in all manner of confusion. By way of showing how deeply habituated we have become to this critical attitude, and, at the same time, how close this brings us to a skeptical cast of mind, we shall take a short but instructive detour on our way to the philosophical revolution of René Descartes.

3. DESCARTES: THE UNIVERSE DOUBTED

Anyone who has surveyed the great burgeoning of publications on Eastern thought in recent times will have either read such a book, or else absorbed the content through another medium. Most everyone, in one way or another, makes their own "Journey to the East." I remark on this and cite the following example only because a frequently highlighted teaching of the East (at least one presented as such) curiously converges with the typical point of departure of much modern Western philosophy. And it has to do precisely with our original attitude towards the world.

One such popular presentation of the major Eastern schools of thought makes a point of showing their positions to stand in uncanny agreement with the most recent findings of physics. Behind these underscored congruities one can detect as tacitly presupposed this new modern attitude toward the world as we first perceive it. The book is the popular *The Tao of Physics* by Fritjof Capra, first published in 1975. It has been controversial, to say the least (as have Capra's later works), but its presentation of the parallels I am addressing is spot on. He writes in his short summation of Hindu doctrine:

> The basic recurring theme in Hindu mythology is the creation of the world by the self-sacrifice of God—"sacrifice" in the original sense of "making sacred"—whereby God becomes the world which, in the end, becomes again God. This creative activity of the Divine is called *lila*, the play of God, and the world is seen as the stage of the divine play. . . . The word *maya* . . . came to signify the psychological state of anybody under the spell of magic play. As long as we confuse the myriad forms of the divine *lila* with reality, without perceiving the unity of Brahman underlying all these forms, we are under the spell of *maya*. *Maya*, therefore, does not mean that the world is an illusion, as is often wrongly stated. The illusion merely lies in our point of view, if we think that the shapes and structures, things and events, around us are realities of nature, instead of realizing that they are concepts of our measuring and categorizing minds. *Maya* is the illusion of taking these concepts for reality, of confusing the map with the territory.[13]

Capra certainly presents us with a more nuanced understanding of *maya* than simply asserting: "The Hindus think the world is not really there." I wonder, however, if it in fact says much more. The word "illusion" itself derives from the Latin word for "play" (*ludere*). And if the divine *lila* accounts for the state of *maya* by putting us under its spell and leading us to "think that the shapes and structures, things and events, around us are realities of nature" when they are not, someone is being fooled.

The author would likely respond that we are indeed the ones who are being fooled, but only as long as we think we exist separately from "the world," and that we constitute

13. Fritjof Capra, *The Tao of Physics*, 2nd ed. (New York: Bantam Books, 1984), 77–78.

anything more than a minor element in its process. He continues:

> As long as our view of the world is fragmented, as long as we are under the spell of *maya* and think that we are separated from our environment and can act independently, we are bound by *karma*. . . . To be free from the spell of *maya*, to break the bonds of *karma*, means to realize that all the phenomena we perceive with our senses are part of the same reality. It means to experience, concretely and personally, that everything, including our own self, is Brahman. This experience is called *moksha*, or "liberation," in Hindu philosophy and it is the very essence of Hinduism.[14]

This all sounds harmless enough to the educated modern reader. He is too inured to current scientific and philosophical ideologies to be disturbed by this one. On the walls of his imagination one already finds the travel plans of a voyage exceeding the speed of light—departing this morning and arriving last night. Nor has he any quarrels with curved space, black holes, or a fourth dimension. And amoebas evolving into nuclear physicists are for him as blasé as polliwogs turning into frogs. Why should he suddenly revolt and hotly insist on thinking that the shapes and structures, the things and events around him are realities of nature, and not just concepts of his measuring and categorizing mind?

One reason why he does not revolt is that the leading thinkers of the modern Western world have already been saying as much for these last 400 years. In our 20th century, the claim has succeeded in working its way down from the universities and learned journals into the sodden fields of everyday platitude. How often do phrases like these reach our ears: "Finally, everything is relative anyway," or "This is true for me, though others may see it differently," or "It all depends upon your point of view." The smoothest and most

14. Ibid., 78–79.

recent causeway for these galloping new creeds has been the well-publicized x-ray vision of the universe offered us by the nuclear physicists.

Indeed Mr. Capra eagerly points this out. He informs us that

> a consistent view of the world is beginning to emerge from modern physics which is harmonious with ancient Eastern wisdom.... Eastern mysticism provides a consistent and beautiful philosophical framework which can accommodate our most advanced theories of the physical world.[15]

Precisely the point where this "beautiful philosophical framework" begins to be drawn as a new setting for the "concepts of our measuring and categorizing minds" is the point at which modern Western philosophy began. It is precisely the point of departure we mentioned at the beginning.

I am not referring to the formal articulation of particular doctrines here, but rather to an underlying presupposition that is summarily accepted and seldom seriously examined in its own right. It is the point of departure of a certain kind of thought—an almost ascetical habit of the mind's pre-scientific training. In the West, such thought was first undertaken in a systematic way by René Descartes in the 17th century, but it can be shown to have existed, our author assures us, from time immemorial in the mysterious East. We are witnessing today its consummation in certain interpretations of modern scientific knowledge. But the first classic utterance of the new presupposition in the West is found in the first of Descartes's famous *Meditations on First Philosophy.* The *Meditations* are, no less than the practices of the same name in St. Ignatius of Loyola's *Spiritual Exercises*, designed to purify the mind of a kind of evil. But the evil targeted here is not moral fault, but rather intellectual error;

15. Ibid., xx.

and the tempter is not the Devil, but, as we shall see, an even more insidious charmer: the world.

⊕

Having determined that all philosophical confusion and error is the result of unexamined and unfounded opinions and personal distortions, Descartes resolves to purge his mind of all such influences in a kind of retreat. Though the passages are well known, they welcome a fresh look in order to isolate our topic:

> I will therefore make a serious and unimpeded effort to destroy generally all my former opinions . . . reason already convinces me that I should abstain from the belief in things which are not entirely certain and indubitable no less carefully than from the belief in things which appear to me to be manifestly false.[16]

Out to make a clean slate, free of all error and confusion, he resolves to start at the source of it all. It is here that we discover the great point of departure, and the focus of our inquiry:

> I shall first attack the principles upon which all my former opinions were founded. Everything which I have thus far accepted as entirely true and assured has been acquired from the senses or by means of the senses. But I have learned by experience that these senses sometimes mislead me. . . .[17]

He then considers the various sources of illusion and deception to which sense experience is prey. He claims to discover that his only refuge from such uncertainties is the assurance which his faith gave him of the good God, who

16. René Descartes, *Discourse on Method and Meditations*, trans. by Laurence Lafleur (New York: Library of Liberal Arts, 1960), 75.

17. Ibid., 76.

would not allow all those perceptions to occur if there were not a real world out there to which they corresponded. However, when that last plank is itself predictably blasted by methodical doubt, our philosopher shrinks back from the shapes and structures, things and events of the world of nature touched by his senses, and utters that low, unchanging drone of cosmic doubt that has haunted modern thought ever since. In his own words:

> I feel sure that I cannot overdo this distrust, since it is not now a question of acting, but only of meditating and learning. I will therefore suppose that, not God, who is very good and who is the supreme source of truth, but a certain evil spirit, not less clever and deceitful than powerful, has bent all his efforts to deceiving me. I will suppose that the sky, the air, the earth, colors, shapes, sounds, and all other objective things that we see are nothing but illusions and dreams that he has used to trick my credulity. I will consider myself as having no hands, no eyes, no flesh, no blood, nor any senses, yet falsely believing that I have all these things. I will remain resolutely attached to this hypothesis; and if I cannot attain the knowledge of any truth by this method, at any rate it is in my power to suspend my judgment. . . .[18]

Of course, what Descartes proposes here is not a formal philosophical teaching as such, but rather the canonization of a new point of departure: the very possibility of assuming a philosophical attitude that seriously doubts the existence of the external world. It is no use pointing out that Descartes himself believed in its existence and is only introducing a method for gauging certitude. Even if just a "thought experiment," it is one which will cast a shadow over that thought even after the experiment is over. He may not have meant

18. Ibid., 8.

that the world is not here, but he did mean that one could begin philosophizing without accepting that it is. And that was as unheard-of in the West as starting to cook with a flippant indifference to the existence of meat, vegetables, and flour. This innovation set a ball rolling which has grown into quite serious and systematic denials of extra-mental reality. In its train have come elaborations of attempted metaphysics seeming to emulate certain "acosmic" interpretations of Hinduism, so much so that one can understand how a great Indologist could write:

> The problem of the "external world," which has only become a basic theme of research in Europe since Descartes, has stood in the center of philosophical discussion in India from the earliest times. . . .[19]

It is often forgotten that Descartes's method of universal doubt and his famous *cogito* were only presented in 1637. He turned in this new direction through a series of events we shall examine in a kind of retrogressive investigation. We have begun with this strange fruit of Descartes's thought, and the precedent he set for both Kant and Husserl in upholding the possibility of not beginning philosophy with a look at the world. Let us now work our way back through the difficult genesis of such an unnatural assumption, and try to find the light that begot this dark.

Again, one thing must be made clear. Descartes was not led to doubt the world by any gnawing second-thoughts about its existence. He was as unworried about that as anyone else. As a matter of fact, at the beginning, his most cherished intellectual project had been not to teach the world about doubt, but to teach doubt about the world. He had proposed to publish his own synthetic philosophy of the

19. Helmuth von Glasenapp, *Die Philosophie der Inder* (Stuttgart: Kréner Verlag, 1958), 451 [my translation].

cosmos, nursing our minds from its blighting incertitude in a work entitled precisely *The World* (*Le Monde*). It is a strange irony that the man who has taught us how to doubt the world's existence wanted originally to do nothing but write a big book *about* the world. Descartes was excited by the new advances in the sciences, and particularly stimulated by his own success in interpreting continuous quantity in terms of discrete. This last was the basis of his contribution to the development of analytic geometry. He was thus inspired to seek a supreme *mathesis universalis*, a *scientia admirabilis*, uniting all the sciences of the cosmos into a synthetic, mathematically articulated system.

The early 17th century, however, saw not only the telescope and the *Starry Messenger* of Galileo. It also witnessed the 30-Years' War and a wake of ecclesiastical anxiety following the first great cleavages of the Reformation. Much of this heaved itself obtrusively upon the interesting researches of the irritable Italian physicist we just named. The story is complex, but its barest outline helps us to understand why Descartes resolved not to publish his *World*. By 1633 the draft was finished. As if by Providence, the news arrived that Galileo had in that same year been freshly rebuked by Rome. *The World*, like Galileo's *Dialogues* (of 1632), presumed the truth of Copernican heliocentrism, and could conceivably have caused Descartes a similar contest with Church authorities. So he put the manuscript away.

Six years prior to this, Cardinal Bérulle, founder of the Oratory of St. Phillip Neri in Paris, had heard Descartes logically refute a new philosophical theory with such precision and confidence that he promptly urged the gifted mathematician to turn his obvious gifts to the reformation of philosophy. The scholasticism of the day was falling into increasing discredit, and a philosophical underpinning of the new scientific discoveries was sadly lacking. It must have seemed to Descartes that the Cardinal had been sent by God, for an event of eight years before *that* was still glowing in his memory, and the Cardinal's words strangely dovetailed with it.

It had been in 1619 that an interior watershed was crossed in the young Frenchman's mind. He had always been strongly attracted to mathematics ever since studying under the Jesuits at La Flêche. In fact, that was the only part of the long and full curriculum that had left a lasting, positive impression upon his mind. Continuing his studies afterwards, he began to realize that he possessed a real aptitude for mathematical imagination and insight. Then came his burning bush. Almost ten years before the Cardinal tapped him on the shoulder, it seemed that the Almighty Himself had called his name.

Descartes was serving in the Catholic army of the Duke of Bavaria in one of the exchanges of the aforementioned war. While holding out for the winter in November, 1619, he resolved to pass the months alone with his thoughts, and to follow the star of his mathematical endowments. He closed himself up in a small house heated by a large brick oven (the famous *poêle*). One evening, in what seems to have been a flash of insight, he saw the key to effecting an homogenization of discrete and continuous quantity by the use of a new method: on coordinates of two straight lines, curved lines could be plotted, assigning numerical values to each point on the curved lines, and thus correlating them with the straight lines. Three powerful dreams that night provided an adequate symbolic alphabet for the somewhat forced construal of a great calling. A vision arose before his eyes: what a method had just done to unite algebra and geometry (allowing the numerical manipulation of the hitherto so-evasive continuum), a method could one day do to unite all the sciences (allowing the technological manipulation of hitherto so-elusive matter). And Descartes felt that he was the man to set the method in motion.

Such was the oneiric appointment. Descartes, who had

already resolved at graduation from the Jesuit academy never to rely on books again, but to read instead in "the book of the world," had become a sort of vagrant. After the Cardinal's confirming words in 1627, he moved to Holland, where he spent most of his remaining years. He still moved around (18 changes of address!); but his pen moved too, for it was there that he wrote his books.

I should say *most* of his books. There was one that he had penned during the 1620's and which was to join his *World* in a corner of his suitcase and be published only in 1701, fifty-two years after his death. This is the famous *Rules for the Direction of the Mind*, an apparently incomplete work with twenty-four rules which offer a method for the hygienic breeding of clear, distinct ideas—like microbes in a laboratory. Exactly why he never published it we do not know. Probably the work was never quite clear enough. In any case, it is curiously appropriate for the purpose of our study that precisely the *World* and the *Rules* were dragged by Descartes from each one of those 18 dwellings to the other, and never hit the market. He was scared by the Church from showing the world his *World*. I fancy he was scared by his own rules from showing the world his *Rules*.

Now these three factors—his 1619 inspiration, the Cardinal's prompting, and Galileo's condemnation—combined to inflame, condense and miniaturize Descartes's almost Newtonian ambitions into the more modest and far more subtle form of a philosophical preface. The *Rules* and *The World* he kept hidden—almost like an esoteric corpus with which only his fully initiated mind could engage—and to the public at large he extended a tripartite sampling of the latter (the *Optics*, the *Meteorology*, and the famous *Geometry*, propounding the development of his 1619 discovery), prefaced by a quickly written, semi-autobiographical discourse. Therein he condensed the two dozen precepts of the *Rules* into a mere four, giving to the opusculum the equally prefatory, unpretentious title: "Discourse on Method." This proemial and entirely propadeutical little discourse (a mere seventh of the book's bulk) promptly and surprisingly reared itself up, atop the centuries, as the watershed of traditional and modern philosophical reflection.

Descartes was to write only two more major works: one, the important *Meditations on First Philosophy* (1641), merely expands on the fourth and pivotal part of the *Discourse*; the other, *The Principles of Philosophy* (1644), does the same again, but adds at long last a fuller treatment of the scientific questions he so yearned to discuss. One presumes that the temperatures had dropped somewhat in the Copernican controversy (Galileo had died in 1642). Still, shortly after Descartes's death his own works were to be put on the Index for a time. But despite the man's enthusiasm for his scientific work, and the attention and consternation of his contemporaries over the same, posterity has looked past all this unbaked science—including his posthumously published *World*—and fixed its fascinated eye on his little preface and his almost mystical meditations.

One word in particular assumed pre-eminence and has since exercised the highest office of supreme philosophical arbiter: the word "method." So here we are. It was using this instrumental method that the big world Descartes so loved, and about which he yearned to write, paradoxically became the object of his own infectious and blighting doubt. *The World* remains on our library shelves, as it did on Descartes's. The *Discourse*, however, is dog-eared by the nervous fingers of scores of modern philosophers, all teased by a new and tenacious disquiet.

Now, the similarity between Descartes's thought and Eastern thought may seem to exhaust itself in this new attitude to the world of sense experience. This is, however, in the strictest sense only a "point of departure." For Descartes, it is canonized in the famous "method of universal doubt." As we shall later see, this starting point has an inner dynamism toward a resolution quite unsuspected by this devout Catholic.

His intention is, as it will later be the intention of Kant, to rescue traditional philosophical and moral truths by giving them an up-to-date scientific vindication. But even the next step of his philosophy betrays the direction his chosen principle is moving in. Applying the strongest and most universal doubt possible, Descartes hoped to see it laid low by the strongest and most universal certitude. But, without even an attempt at justification—having already maintained the wisdom of doubting the world's existence—his mind feels free to demand that all certitude measure up to the two criteria of his favorite science: mathematics. Those two criteria are clarity and precision. In the welter of humanistic scholarship with which his professors had cloyed him, and the tediously commentated *sententiae* of scholasticism (more Suarezian than Thomistic, one should add), the advances in mathematics and its potential developments arose like an immense crystal chandelier before his eyes—clear, sparkling and shedding light on everything. Descartes's own contribution to geometry sealed his enthusiasm with a personal investment. The conspicuous way in which mathematics slips into the philosophical scenario is indicative of much that is to come. A few clarifications about this discipline will be apropos before we can understand its peculiar fascination for René Descartes.

Excursus No. 1: On Mathematics

Galileo said that "the book of nature is written in mathematical characters." That was the book Descartes had set out to read. He discovered he was fluent in the language, and could read fast. I fear it was too fast. But let us have a look at the language.

Mathematics has always enjoyed a privileged position in Western education, and for good reason. The Greek word derives from a verb meaning simply "to learn." It is the first and most teachable of the sciences, requiring minimal experience in the world of things, but is eminently lucid, in its initial articulations easy to grasp, and productive of a satisfying, once-and-for-all certitude. But the very subject-matter of math, for all its certitude, suffers one serious handicap. The objects of mathematics are indifferent to existence, and obey a kind of order that is dissociated from finality and devoid of motion. The fundamental ideas are clearly intuited at the outset, and all that follows is logic.

And what is this docile and lucid subject-matter? It is the relationship between quantities, and quantity itself is the primary accident of material substances; through it, and it alone, is material substance, with all its qualities, made manifest to the senses. The red of the rose will vanish if it lacks at least a few square inches in which to show itself off. The scholastics say that quantity is the *measure* of the substance, meaning that by which the substance is known. Quantity as an accident is not studied by mathematics, but, in the Aristotelian scheme, by metaphysics, for quantity is a kind of accident modifying the being of material substances. It is also examined in natural philosophy as a factor in mobile being, making motion possible to begin with. What, then, is left over for the mathematician? Precisely the relationships between quantities. In a quantitative, mathematical order, all parts are homogeneous, differing from one another only in situation and calculation; thus their relationships alone are of interest.

The very primacy of quantity among the accidents enables its study to be of such scope. Through mathematics you can learn something about all material beings, namely, the ways in which they are all quantitatively measurable and interrelated. Quantity is a real accident out in the extra-mental world, and in natural philosophy and metaphysics, that real quantity is considered. The natural philosopher, exercising the most elementary mode of abstraction, abstracts his object, mobile being, from the conditions of individuality only, and thus regards quantity as still serving as a support for qualities. The metaphysician, however, separates his object, being *as being*, from all individual and sensory conditions; for he is interested in quantity only as one of the nine accidents that can modify that which truly is, namely, substance. Thus, the natural philosopher resolves his knowledge about quantity into judgments terminating in his sense experience, whereas the metaphysician resolves his knowledge about quantity into judgments terminating in his intellectual grasp of being.

The mathematician's conclusions about quantitative relations terminate neither in the real world, nor in his intellect as such, but in his imagination. There never exists a perfect correspondence between those abstracted integers and figures in his imagination and the bodies in the world. There is, however, enough of a correspondence to make the discipline immensely helpful in understanding that world, and, especially for modern man, in manipulating it. The science itself, however, remains perfectly abstract, perfectly formal—so much so that it welcomes all sorts of original speculations and fanciful configurations. It is precisely this creative, projective use of the mathematical imagination that plays such a crucial role in the experimental method.

The mathematical object's formal disengagement from matter (that notorious matrix of contingency and change) enables it to be defined without matter; nonetheless, it is unable to exist without matter. Now, once quantities are regarded as existing, they are once again supporting qualities, thus involved in all the imprecisions of the real, and requiring the two sciences of the real we just mentioned. So the mathematician's object is something that does not, that cannot exist in the form in which it is studied. The sort of quasi-existence it enjoys in the imagination is the result of the constructive work of the reason performed on the "intelligible matter" of the imagination. Since we are ourselves, in a sense, the creators of these little triangles and equations, we are able to have a supreme and exhaustive understanding of them. After all, there can only be a virtual distinction between their essences and their properties. Once I know that a triangle is a plane figure bounded by three straight lines, I can deduce all its properties, with no need to go out into the world and broaden my experience of triangles through additional observation. The definition is perfectly intelligible, because the defined is perfectly imaginative.

Of course the trueness to reality of a given mathematical object can only be tested by returning to the material order, as in the experimental verification of mathematical hypotheses. But the clearly deduced conclusions mathematical reason yields apply in their full precision only to the objects as they exist immaterially in the imagination. Aristotle accordingly will insist that math should never lose its reference to the physical order, from which it is abstracted, and the understanding of which it ought, therefore, to serve.[20]

As material things are full of contingency and evasive of definitive scientific coverage, this uniquely abstract quality of mathematics enables us to achieve a clarity and precision possible in no other science. And the universality of mathematics (in regard, at least, to the material world) makes it easy prey for those who are weary of the verbose efforts of the other two universal intellectual disciplines: logic and metaphysics. These two deal with objects that are indifferent to matter not only in definition, but also in existence.

Logic, however, deals only with the second intentions of the mind—"beings of reason," such as genera, specific differ-

20. Aristotle, *Metaphysics* III, 996a 34; XIII 1076b 11 (McKeon edition).

ences, predicables, etc., capable only of intra-mental existence—and studies the order among concepts. Metaphysics, on the other hand, deals with being *as being*, and is a true science of the real in pursuit of the knowledge of this subject in the light of its ultimate cause; thus, it deals with first intentions, i.e., concepts and judgments "intending" a real extramental being or event (e.g., a cause, matter and form, substance, act, etc.). Now both these disciplines were to undergo considerable 17th-century revampings. Indeed, while Descartes was "communing with his thoughts" beside the *poéle* in 1619, Francis Bacon was preparing to publish his *Novum Organum*, intending to shoulder Aristotelian logic off the map of the modern mind. And when Descartes put a rubber band around his *World* in 1633, it was not too far away, in Amsterdam, that a Jewish boy was born who was to be the first notable metaphysician of the modern world: Baruch Spinoza. Neither of these disciplines, however, were ready to serve as a new universal groundwork for Descartes's ambitious project. At least not yet. But mathematics, newly empowered by Descartes's own innovations, seemed perfectly tailored for the job.

⊕

Descartes's philosophical revolution set out to replace the unmanageable, notoriously imprecise world our senses touch with a crystal-clear *kosmos noetos* of ideas, modeled after the paradigm of mathematics. Beginning with clear, intellectual intuitions of ideas, all knowledge worthy of the name would be "deduced" by a series of carefully controlled derivative intuitions.

The result of this erection of a mathematical paradigm is well known. The practitioner of methodic doubt shakes his head in the face of all but intellectual intuitions, leading our philosopher to desperately seek an idea that, together with clarity and precision, also connotes existence. Unfortunately for Descartes, the very first ideas he must disqualify are all the ideas of mathematics, for there is not a number or a geometric figure whose clear, distinct idea bespeaks existence. The sole suggestion of real existence turns out to be an intuited deduction of his own real existence based on nothing else beyond the undeniable fact of his own real doubt. This leads him to accept only the existence of his own doubting self as certain, and then to exalt the parameters of that certitude into the absolute standard for all certitude. To doubt, however, is to think. To think is to be involved in an act which presupposes an existing subject of the act. We who think have found the thinker, and behold, he exists!—"I think, therefore I am."

Finally, for Descartes, doubt must capitulate before an inner sanctum of supreme intellectual evidence: the evidence of the ego. This high throne of conviction is of such pristine lucidity precisely because it is free from all sensory derivation, and all the obscuring opacity of matter. We have climbed above the clouds of the tricky world and found the primordial light of the mind. One is reminded of Plato's prisoner who escaped from the cave of shadows into the sunlight, only afterwards to return to his imprisoned fellows to tell them about the world of light. Now Descartes too takes a deep breath and proceeds to step forth out of this rarefied atmosphere of indubitability and re-descend into the mortal world where all of us woolly thinkers dwell. Now, however, he is proudly holding aloft this newly charged intuitional klieg light that will enable the whole world to be clearly, distinctly and philosophically filmed for the first time in history.

The first requirement to be imposed upon that world which Descartes is now re-approaching is that it be susceptible to the penetration of this *res cogitans*, that is, the self-conscious knowing subject, and that it do this by sharing some quality of like clarity and precision. However, Descartes suddenly stops in his tracks, as if stunned by an unexpected, Johnny-come-lately doubt. And yet, upon examination, it is no new doubt, but rather the second-born certitude of his initial doubt. He had doubted his way to certitude about himself; now that same doubt reminds him that a second light of unquestionable fact is packaged up in that first uncertainty.

Whoever doubts, you see, and is *sure* that he is doubting, knows that he is performing a defective sort of act, which necessarily implies something more perfect; this, in turn, means that we have an idea of perfection. Now this idea, too, can be X-rayed with intellectual intuition and be shown to include the note of existence. After all, could ultimate Perfection be what we think it to be, if it were non-existent? Of course not, answers Descartes, thus giving his own spin to the famous "ontological argument" for the existence of God. This need not detain us further. Important for Descartes is only that God's existence be clearly and distinctly ascertained *first*, for without His almighty help, we will be unable to find our way back down this mountain of vision to the solid world we left behind.

Step three: We had no difficulty seeing the clarity and precision of the mathematical idea of extension. But we were unable to begin with it because the idea exhausts its lucid content without a hint of real existence. But now, Descartes asserts, that problem is solved. Our philosopher coyly remarks—like a man suddenly feigning polite surprise at the presence of company he had tried to ignore—that his soul is, as a matter of fact, jumping and stomping with all sorts of sense-impressions. And what is more, he is, as are we all, oddly inclined to regard these sensations as hailing from an extra-mental world.

The august marriage of mind and reality, into which earlier philosophers had leapt with a kind of unchaste zest, could now be properly solemnized by none other than God

Himself. (Remember, the Godhead is present by proxy in the clear, distinct idea we have of Him!) Upon further analysis of the idea of God, one discovers veracity to be among the attributes of perfection. Now He who created us and the world, being an honest God, would not allow us to be led astray by such suasive sensations. Thus, they must be trustworthy. At this grave and ceremonial moment, a "thinking thing" and an "extended thing" are pronounced husband and wife. With a thump of apodictic conviction, we have landed again on Planet Earth.

Let us reduce Descartes's method to its essential content. Through an ingenious psychology of certitude, the French philosopher attempts to establish indubitability in the cognition of reality through a functional analysis of the cogitation of ideas. Cognition is necessarily *of something*, and such things vex us with their multiplicity, mutability, contingency, and, above all, imprecision. Cogitation, however, is a process of the mind, and as such would seem to submit to the same mechanical scrutiny as any other process, its laws be studied and its first button-push discovered.

This was the start of modern philosophy. No longer are we to be at the mercy of the world and its riot of things, trying in vain to *know* them. From now on, fired by the prophetic dream of René Descartes, the things of the world will be at the mercy of a mind that knows itself at last, and is able to use its machinery like a fine-precision instrument in the supreme art of "having ideas." But the new method will soon betray a curious impotence in one area. The minds of the masters of this new art soon look like palimpsests of a daydreaming demiurge, for the unintended upshot of placing the "having of ideas" before the "knowing of things" is that the idea of the world around us turns out to be the hardest of all ideas to have.

4. KANT: THE UNIVERSE POSTULATED

Descartes ushered in the new point of departure, and the greater lot of philosophers followed suit. Though many variations were ventured, the list of possibilities is quite finite. Chesterton somewhere comments on the contrasting moods we find in two works of his intellectual foe, H.G. Wells: first, in the early study of "Doubts of the Instrument," we have before us an epistle of cheerful skepticism, and then in one of his very last works, *The Mind at the End of its Tether*, a limp capitulation of all mental ambition. The thorough skepticism Wells pursued, following out the consequences of Descartes's point of departure, pressed his universe painfully together. Wells's chosen image is telling, for the doubts available to the skeptic do not open up like a broadening horizon but do indeed work like the short tether of a nervous dog, running in circles as he winds his little universe into smaller and smaller rings of captivity.

Kant's variation on the new point of departure is, of course, the most impressive, and has extended itself over the Western mind like a new Holy Roman Empire of the German Nation—though it has been far more successful than that empire ever was. Kant's work came a century-and-a-half after Descartes, and a century after Isaac Newton, the man who really accomplished what Descartes had originally intended (the second edition of *The Critique of Pure Reason* appeared in 1787, 100 years after Newton's *Mathematical Principles of Natural Philosophy*). Kant's *Critique* also came fifty years after David Hume's *Treatise on Human Nature*. Kant is thus free of the premature scientific pretenses of Descartes, is schooled in the proven system of Newton, and sobered (indeed deeply unsettled) by the skeptical questions of Hume. But in all this, he is still filled with confidence that refusing to accept the universe at its first self-introduction is as firmly entrenched a modern achievement as is the discovery of the Americas or of the circulation of the blood. More significantly yet, Kant is not only beyond Descartes chronologically (and in the modern world, that is already a high distinction), but he is also beyond him geographically. Kant was an enlightened German, and the philosophical future belonged to the Germans.

Descartes, still a convinced Catholic, was full of France and all the glories of Gallic lucidity. After him and his epigone, Nicholas Malebranche, no more would a Roman Catholic, and none but one or two Frenchmen, succeed in shaking the world with their ideas. Kant's cool and only collaterally Christian philosophy came in a package starkly contrasting with the succinct, polished French and Latin of Descartes. Here, instead, was that convoluted, heavily periodic and suggestively graphic idiom that Martin Luther's *Bible* had heralded from the Saxon chancery and into the standard stream of written *Hochdeutsch*. Kant's long-matured reflections poured themselves voluminously into the machinery of that language, and his huge *Critique of Pure Reason* had a philosophical impact unequaled by anything since Descartes's laconic *Discourse*.

Some further contrasts between these two philosophical kinsmen are worth noting. We spoke of Descartes's constant meandering. Kant, however, is famous for staying home. And his home, significantly, was in the easternmost corner of Western Europe. I suspect few realize that Kant's home, Königsberg is now Kaliningrad, the principal Russian seaport on the Baltic. Kant stayed home in northern Prussia, and in his mind, directed the intellectual itinerary of all the Europe he would never visit. From that same quarter of the continent, a horde of Prussian soldiers was to emerge in the coming century, and then their descendents write the libretto for the tragedy of the 20th. Together with the more southerly German tribes, Prussia had never been Romanized in antiquity. But unlike those southern Germans, its Christianization did not come with St. Boniface in the 9th century, but 400 years later in the bloody conquests of the 13th-century Teutonic Knights. And when they went Protestant, just three centuries later, any symbiosis with the deeper resources of Latin Christendom was rapidly checked.

Nonetheless, the Prussians did turn, as they always do, to the south and to the west for a tutor. Whom they received, though, was dictated by the new confusions afflicting the continent in the modern era. All examples one could cite are summed up perfectly by Frederick the Great's repeated and pressing invitation to Voltaire to come and teach at his court, which Voltaire finally accepted in 1750. That friendship cooled fast, but the urbane French rationalism fell on eager Prussian ears. And after being ground through the mental machinery of German Idealism, it was one day to descend anew upon Europe with a vengeance.

Kant may thus be characterized as the philosopher who absorbed the late, disordered intellectual produce of Western Europe and recast it all in his own sprawling system—supremely methodical and exhaustive, but forbiddingly complicated and abstruse, presuming, without so much as a pose of humility, to lay bare the hidden enginery of all human thought. These lines appear at the opening of *The Critique of Pure Reason*:

> I flatter myself that I have, in this way, discovered the cause of—and consequently the mode of removing—all the errors which have hitherto set reason at variance with itself, in the sphere of non-empirical thought. . . . My chief aim in this work has been thoroughness; and I make bold to say that there is not a single metaphysical problem that does not find its solution, or at least the key to its solution here.[21]

KANT

21. *The Critique of Pure Reason*, Preface to first ed., trans. by J.M.D. Meiklejohn, from *Great Books of the Western World*, vol. 42 (Chicago: University of Chicago Press, 1952), 2.

Unlike Descartes, Kant hardly ever began to truly philosophize. But it makes little difference, for, like Descartes's, his influence on posterity is limited largely to his propadeutical, epistemological orientation. It's all ground-work, and acres of it.

Nor is Kant as readily epitomized as Descartes, and we shall not even attempt it. At any rate, it is only his incipient decision not to begin with the affirmation of the existence of the world behind sense experience that concerns us in our treatment of Chesterton. This much we can, however inadequately, summarize.

Kant is just as little a solipsist, or acosmist, as Descartes was. He will kick a pine-cone out of his path just as anyone else would as he takes his famous daily walk through the streets of Königsberg. But when he returns from his walk, and sits back down to his writing desk, he will re-enter that strange hollow of the brain to which Descartes withdrew when he closed the doors on the Bavarian winter and snuggled up beside the *poéle*, all alone with his thoughts.

Let us gather, as we did with Descartes, a small sampling of our philosopher's conclusions regarding our first encounter with the universe. Toward the end of the first *Critique*, when Kant finally turns to consider our cognitive stance over against the universe as a whole, this is what he says (forgive the length of the quote—I don't want to be accused of cherry-picking; the very complication of Kant's train of thought here is evidence of what happens when you try to *reason* your way to the world):

> I term all transcendental ideas, in so far as they relate to the absolute totality in the synthesis of phenomena, *cosmical conceptions*, partly on account of this unconditioned totality, on which the conception of the world-whole is based—a conception, which is itself an idea—partly because they relate solely to the synthesis of phenomena—the empirical synthesis; while, on the other hand, the

> absolute totality in the synthesis of the conditions of all possible things gives rise to an idea of pure reason, which is quite distinct from the cosmical conception, although it stands in relation with it.[22]
>
> [T]he cosmological idea is either too great or too small for the empirical regress in a synthesis, and consequently for every possible conception of the understanding. . . .
>
> We are thus led to the well-founded suspicion that the cosmological ideas, and all the conflicting sophistical assertions connected with them, are based upon a false and fictitious conception of the mode in which the object of these ideas is presented to us; and this suspicion will probably direct us how to expose the illusion that has so long led us astray from the truth.[23]
>
> The sensuous world contains nothing but phenomena, which are mere representations, and always sensuously conditioned; *things in themselves are not, and cannot be, objects to us.*[24] [emphasis added]

Descartes had subjected the world to doubt; Kant subjects our knowledge of it to a critique. With every intention of affirming its existence, his critique of pure reason ends by giving our knowledge of cosmic existence the status of a mere "regulative idea," to which nothing corresponds in our objective experience. How is it that Kant could arrive at this remarkable conclusion? (Before continuing, the reader is asked to lift his eyes from the page and look out a window at the sky and the busy world stretched out beneath it—*that* is the big universe that is under discussion.)

We shall first consider a family of influences which bore upon Kant's life and thought in significant ways. The Reformation, to begin with, had left an obvious mark. One of the early metamorphoses of Lutheran *sola-fideism* was the Pietist

22. Ibid., 130.
23. Ibid., 153.
24. Ibid., 172.

sect, stressing a non-dogmatic, interior turning to the Lord, and a severely pointed insistence on the supremacy of moral rectitude over intellectual pretension. Kant's mother and early Latin teacher had impressed the stoic and anti-dogmatic spirit of this sect upon the mind of little Immanuel.

Rationalism was also to fill his early decades through his university training in the philosophy of Leibniz, as artificially codified and scholasticized by Christian Wolff and Alexander Baumgarten. Overweening confidence in the embracing capacities of reason carried Kant into the rushing and expanding current of the 18th-century Enlightenment, eager to touch, purify, and illuminate all the confused and tangled heaps of thought that Western man had hitherto produced.

Jean-Jacques Rousseau's moral sentimentalism was to recast and underpin Kant's Pietistic moral earnestness. The only recorded exception to the philosopher's illustriously accurate 5 p.m. daily strolls were the few days he was absorbed in the Frenchman's *Émile*. The staid Prussian was swept out of his clockwork regime by the ardent prose of a man from the heart of a moribund Christendom.

The Revolution in Rousseau's homeland was also to impinge upon Kant's later writings; for though he withdrew his initial support in the face of the Reign of Terror, his philosophical principles on moral law would serve to feed the new revolutionary spirit by laying a new foundation for modern internationalism.

Even the Romanticism of the early 19th century was not without a relationship to Kant's later works, when his somber cogitations turn to art and beauty, and he decrees their emancipation from moral and practical purposiveness.

The Renaissance, however—to move back a couple of centuries—seems to have sent hardly a breeze into the soul of Kant. He did not care for music, or women (he never married), nor did he ever see—or apparently desire to see—all the classical art into which Christianity had breathed a new spirit; he never visited Paris, or Rome, or Vienna, or even Berlin. He stayed home in Prussia. But Kant was—despite the staidness of his writing—a popular teacher, a wide reader, a man fond of entertaining dinner guests (preferring sailors and businessmen to fellow academics), knowledgeable about the world, and esteemed as a gifted conversationalist. It is noteworthy, too, that he regularly gave summer courses in physical geography, perhaps compensating with maps for what he never saw in true landscapes. One could argue that this last serves as an accurate metaphor for his approach to knowledge in general.

But enough of this alliterative assessment of influences! It was neither Reformation nor Rationalism, neither Revolution nor Rousseau that really fired the writing of Immanuel Kant. It was rather the same force that had taken charge of Descartes: the New Science. Descartes wished to serve the cosmos by writing a book about it. Kant wished to render the same service by defending a book that had already been written about it. It was Sir Isaac Newton's *Mathematical Principles of Natural Philosophy*. Upon this masterpiece we must briefly dwell.

Excursus No. 2: On Newton

Even weaker in constitution than the frail Kant, the newborn Newton, it was feared, would not survive his first day. That he did survive has been one of the formative facts of the modern world, and in no small degree because of his influence upon Kant. Now if the 19th century was carried by Kant, the 18th was certainly carried by Newton, perhaps even more than Descartes. Descartes had inspired the new style of philosophy, looking inward, and insisting we begin philosophy with the contents of consciousness, whether with a world of ideas (rationalism) or of sense impressions (empiricism). To Newton, however, had been granted the considerable task, in his *Principles*, of giving an account of the universe lying outside of and somehow beyond these self-scrutinizing subjects.

If Descartes had lived to see this book, he would either have fumed with envy, or fallen to his knees. Here was his *World* at last: a grand, exhaustive panorama of the physical universe, methodically applying mathematics to search out the forces of nature, and then using the mathematical results to explain the phenomena we see, and predict many we have yet to see. The experimental method of Galileo and the analytical geometry of Descartes himself had made the study of nature more and more susceptible to mathematical treatment. The experimental method utilized a mathematical *medium sciendi* (means of knowledge), permitting the behavior of matter to be calculated in numbers. And that medium grew more refined as the decades of the 17th century passed.

The new geometry tamed the native intellectual obstruction of continuous quantity and its incommensurable magnitudes by tying it onto the Cartesian graph of neat and straight coordinates. Furthermore, Galileo's new mathematical understanding of motion enabled one to think of it not as an act, but as a state. Enlisting the services of the concept of inertia, this innovation had made it feasible to study all of nature—and this included what one had hitherto gathered under the fearful rubrics of acts and causes, forms and ends—henceforth as clear and distinct states that can be mathematically plotted.

Newton and Leibniz would complete this ensemble of new tools by discovering the infinitesimal calculus, permitting for the first time the mathematical reckoning of that angle of motion which the New Science had chosen: force. Force was a quantitative reworking of the old concept of act, now neatly mathematicized as the product of a body's mass and acceleration. This notion of force denoted the energy

Newton!

needed, not to maintain a body in the state of motion, but to change its state, either accelerating it, or changing it from a state of rest to a state of motion, or *vice versa*. Such a mathematically manageable concept could be used to describe *all* events, integrating the insights into celestial mechanics of Johannes Kepler with those into terrestrial mechanics of Galileo Galilei.

Bringing further clarity and precision were the likewise mathematical concepts of mass (the measure of a body's resistance to acceleration), which in a way replaced the older, philosophical concept of matter, and the mathematical concept of momentum (mass times velocity), as handier than the broader, dimmer concept of motion itself. With the three new concepts of mass, force, and momentum, Newton goes on to expound his famous three laws of motion: 1) the law of inertia; 2) the law of force; and 3) the law of reaction. Applying all this to planetary motion, he arrives at the great universal law of gravitation; and at this mathematical juncture, all the articulations of his vast system touch, and are sequentially charged with lucidity and coherence.

The supremacy of mathematics seemed forever secured. In another accomplishment, Newton seemed almost to be treading on sacred ground when he proposed to interpret light as a complex, heterogeneous phenomenon, analyzable into differing rays, diffracting in mathematically computable manner. He seemed to be turning color—that quality of qualities—into a quantitative reality. Goethe would later vent pages of Romantic indignation against this reduction in his famous *Farbenlehre*.

In brief, this is the background of the scientific revolution that made mathematically measurable states the paragon of reliable knowledge for the new and enlightened age.

⊕

We have spent some time with a summary portrayal of the Newtonian synthesis for two reasons. First, Kant regarded Newton's science as a given, and spent years studying and teaching it. One can say that *The Mathematical Principles of Natural Philosophy*, written at the other end of Europe, inspired Kant more than any other book, even Descartes's "book of the world." Secondly, our topic in this part of the book is the modern philosophical refusal to take the world seriously at one's first encounter with it. Like Descartes, Kant refuses this civility while in the very act of reaching out for a new scientific understanding of that very world.

My thesis is that the only defensible point of departure for sane and coherent philosophy is the imprecise but luminous idea of being and the first principles that it generates. And I hope to show that G.K. Chesterton propounded and defended this truth with unprecedented brilliance. If you do not start at that natural beginning, you have to start (or try to start) somewhere else. Descartes tried to start with universal doubt, and claimed he had then discovered a new point of departure in the *cogito*; he subsequently proceeded to demonstrate the world's existence from that premise. Kant worked his way up to the *cogito* too, but he did not start with doubt. He started with a critique.

Now to start with a critique means that you insist on examining your own faculty of knowledge, its limits and possibilities—setting down the true frontiers of cognition and erecting stoplights at every such border—and to accomplish this in great detail *before* endeavoring to philosophize. Aristotle, on the contrary, taught that man has already begun knowing some things long before he is capable of critiquing anything. Kant will claim that such a one is still in philosophical diapers, a "dogmatist," who takes things on authority and has yet to learn how to use his head. Then there is the "adolescent" skeptic, still in the throes of mental parturition, shocked by a few epistemological disillusionments and unsure of most everything. Kant's mature man, however, is neither dogmatic nor skeptical, but instead *critical.* For him, nothing is accepted except what passes the purity canons of the fully self-conscious reason, grounded in its own inalienable certitude. Such is the Kantian breakdown of the phases of our mental evolution.

The critical philosopher, of course, has to start somewhere too. And my point here is simply that Kant started with the world of Newton's mechanics. He then strangely excluded its overall validity from the critique to which everything else under that Newtonian sun was thoroughly and unsparingly subjected.

In a way, it can be maintained that the place of "the world" in Kant's thought is occupied by the Newtonian mechanics of the cosmos. As we saw with Descartes, it is not really possible *not* to start with the world, but one can quite deftly talk oneself into thinking that one has not. Kant, in starting to think all over again, was convinced that he had found the master-key to such a new beginning. His unreasoned allegiance to Newton's cosmos is merely a lingering echo of a more traditional wisdom in his critical mind. He does treat that mechanical synthesis with the same mental submission with which one ought to treat first principles. That is, he does not inquire *whether* it is true, but only *how.*

In the very first sentence of his *Critique,* he assures us: "That all our knowledge begins with experience there can be no doubt." If he had not forewarned us with his long Preface, we might suspect approaching realism. Kant goes on for a paragraph making this opening statement all the more assertive, and ends with these words: "In respect of time, therefore, no knowledge of ours is antecedent to experience, but begins with it." We are already waving across the centuries at Aristotle and Aquinas, when the next sentence hits us abruptly with a "but" that will detain us for the next 500 pages of the *Critique*. "But, though all our knowledge *begins* with experience, it by no means follows that all *arises* out of experience."[25] [emphases added]

Yes, there is a world out there. And yes, Newton has shown us in magisterial fashion how that world works. But after reading Hume, Kant had realized that the sense experience of man cannot yield up the universality and necessity which Kant, again quite uncritically, has attributed to Newton's conclusions. Granting to that mechanistic universe the unassailable status of a sort of first principle, our philosopher finds himself in the jaws of a dilemma: that mathematical universe of Newton cannot be called evident without making the Englishman's mammoth demonstration of it look rather redundant; on the other hand, it is not deduced from some evident law, but only mathematically worked out from premises drawn forth from Newton's intuitions. So Kant casts about for another anchor of certitude, other than intellectual intuition, other than logical deduction from such intuitions. The source he finds is, again, the critique. He turns his back on that with which Newton's world "begins," and turns a disciplined eye to that from which it "arises." Now if you swallow this last delicate distinction as ostensibly harmless and wholesome, Kant has just put you in his pocket.

The big world "arises" from somewhere whence it does not "begin." Our philosopher is preparing to rescue the necessity and universality of Newtonian science by claiming to discover within the structure of the human mind a built-in apparatus of forms, categories and ideas which are prior to sense experience, and therefore capable of constituting it as experience. They are devoid of the mere contingency and mere associationism of sense impressions because they

25. Ibid., 14.

totally "transcend" them; they are "pure," Kant insists. "Pure of what?" we ask. "Pure of sense experience!" he beams back. These *a priori* forms and categories are necessary and universal because we cannot think anything without them, and sense impressions are like silly putty under their constitutive influence.

The senses alone "intuit" the appearances of physical things by ordering them according to the sensory *a priori* forms of time and space. Those appearances are then further ordered by the "understanding" (*Verstand*), which arranges them according to its similarly *a priori* "categories," following upon its likewise *a priori* judgments. Although the senses are merely receptive of all those impressions, the understanding disposes of a native spontaneity allowing it to dictate the categorical synthesis of predicate and subject in such a way that knowledge occurs and grows. Its formal structure, however, is of the mind's own making. This is really the kernel of Kantianism, and if the man had possessed a wider philosophical culture, embracing a deeper familiarity with Aristotle and Aquinas as well as with Leibniz and Hume, he may have seen that his critique had a quite limited reach. It fully applies only to that new sort of scientific knowledge which followed the paradigms of Galileo and Newton, and is inapplicable to traditional natural philosophy and metaphysics. It is only the New Science which feeds for its livelihood on the projects, hypotheses, and anticipatory constructions of a "spontaneous" understanding.

An adequate and fair exposition of Kant's system would add another thirty pages to this already overgrown chapter. What is of great moment for our purposes is only Kant's claim that *nowhere* in our experience—nowhere accessible to the scientific work of our understanding forming the stuff of our senses—is "the world" to be found. One had refused to start with it, and now may grow panicky at the prospect of having entirely lost sight of it.

But again, not to worry. We can hear Kant's reassuring voice from deep within some streamlined passageway of his transcendental subway: "I have found the world! It exists!" To our somewhat incredulous but hopeful query, "Where?", our philosopher begins a long, seemingly interminable disquisition about three marvelous "ideas" he has found in "reason" (*Vernunft*). For Kant the "reason" is our capacity to *think* what we cannot *know*, and to do this according to "ideas." Reason, in this sense, is to be distinguished from the "understanding" (*Verstand*), which is the faculty involved in *knowing* what we can *experience* according to "categories." Within this *Vernunft* he has found his own version of the three basic Cartesian ideas of God, the soul, and the world. The quote we began with records this curious and superficially reassuring find. But as our mind hovers over these new ideas and wonders what to *do* with them, we are rudely cautioned.

Kant insists that we are absolutely unable to speculatively *know* the realities those ideas purportedly denote. But in the same breath he assures us that we can do the next best thing: we can *think* them. These ideas are, for Kant, certain cogitative inclinations of the reason to think a unified synthesis of the unconditioned as a kind of regulative finality for all the conditioned cognitions of the lower understanding. As with Descartes, cogitation usurps the throne of cognition. For Kant, these three ideas, which form the subject-matter for the three-fold *metaphysica specialis* of Wolff—cosmology, psychology, and natural theology—and hark back to the first "clear and distinct" ideas of Descartes, have to be saved. Otherwise, the other lobe of Kant's brain, that of the moralist, would be left to contemplate moral anarchy on earth all the while Newton's laws rolled smoothly on in the heavens like a placid backdrop to a Euripidean tragedy; for, without these ideas, morality is finished.

But if they are to be saved, Kant tells us, speculative reason

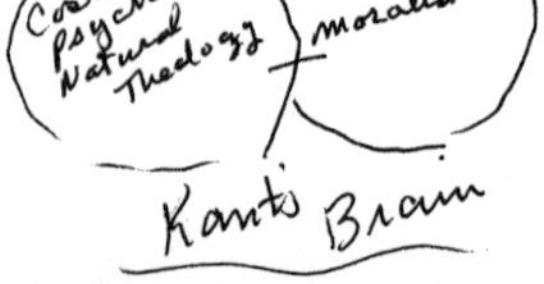

will be of no help. It points feebly at the real world, lying somewhere out there beyond the noise of the senses, but it cannot touch it. It is full of agreeable thoughts about God and an immortal soul, but they are only thoughts and only indirectly have anything to do with knowledge. The salvation we seek will come, we are told, not from speculative but from *practical* reason. For when Kant, in his second *Critique*, turns to the seemingly indubitable moral imperative in the practical reason (another logical gratuity), he discovers that these three ideas of pure reason must needs be *postulated*, in some way, by practical reason.

The root of this is what Kant calls the "categorical imperative" of practical reason, which simply means that reason commands in a purely formal and unconditioned way that the will only want what could be a law for all. This unexamined imperative of duty functions autonomously as the sole moral engine of man, independent of considerations of good, happiness, pleasure, utility, or love. This imperative is "pure," unconditioned, and presupposes that there be an ultimate moral Arbiter (= God), that the moral agent's life extend beyond one severely conditioned life-time (= immortal soul), and... Here we stand again, waiting for the second great modern epistemologist to solemnly restore to our minds, blistered by this long trek of sinuous critique, its long-lost but still-treasured universe. Kant, however, is not going to give it back to us. Listen:

> It is the concept of freedom alone that enables us to find the unconditioned and intelligible for the conditioned and sensible *without going out of ourselves*. [emphasis added] For it is our own reason that by means of the supreme and unconditional practical law knows that itself and the being that is conscious of this law (our own person) belong to the pure world of understanding, and moreover defines the manner in which, as such, it can be active. In this way it can be understood why in the whole faculty of reason it

> is the practical reason only that can help us to pass beyond the world of sense and give us knowledge of a supersensible order and connection, which, however, for this very reason cannot be extended further than is necessary for pure practical purposes.[26]

You see, we do get a "world" back, but it is one that needs those quotation marks around it. It threatens to evaporate without them. Kant's very last writings, published posthumously, betray his own growing perplexity about that new inner universe. The German Idealists, on the other hand, hoisted their sails and charged off, like explorers on the heels of Columbus.

Before considering the third great modern attempt to start philosophy all over again, we need to try and piece together a sort of selective survey of the whole sweep of these three centuries leading up to the 20th-century juncture that saw Chesterton and our third great philosopher, Husserl. If the issue of our study is as central as I suggest, it should aid us in isolating certain crucial lines of development that will help us to fathom the often shapeless preoccupations and anxieties of 20th-century man. This in turn will help us to see Chesterton against a background that is most complimentary to his imposing profile.

Excursus No. 3: The Seeds of the 20th Century

In the century-and-a-half between René Descartes and Immanuel Kant, both the dream of the former and the prophecies of Francis Bacon had all ostensibly found fulfillment in the triumph of Newtonian science. The new approach of Descartes had won over philosophy, though it was the more subdued light of a quite different philosopher,

26. *The Critique of Practical Reason*, from *Great Books of the Western World*, vol. 42, 336.

John Locke, which brightened the path into the 18th-century. Locke was to become its principal pedagogue. All the while the deeper and more faithfully Cartesian speculations of Baruch Spinoza were burrowing busily away; but their very profundity kept them beyond the depth of the age. Europe was too excited by new inventions and easily lured by the vision of a cool, universal reason spreading its pacifying light over all the embattled fields of the age's struggles.

The more diffuse genius of Gottfried Leibniz, full of sketches and projects and letters, better reflects the spirit of the time. The temporary success of his philosophy, as later polished into system by Christian Wolff, was itself evidence that the age was not yet ready for Spinoza. The gifted Jewish metaphysician lived but forty-five years. When he died, however, in 1677, he left the world the truest legacy of the new Cartesian principle. That legacy would be picked up appreciatively by Hegel in the troubled wake of Kant's critique at the opening of the 19th century.

The immediate leanings of late 17th-century thought were to the more down-to-earth offerings of the Anglo-Saxon mind. Bacon had blown the fanfare, and Newton's *Principia* duly marched in procession. It remained only for Locke to lay out the practical program for the *siècle des lumières* to come. We need the French for the stunning clarity of a new idea, the Germans for its elaboration, but we turn to the British for the no-nonsense implementation. The atypical eclecticism of Leibniz's German mind deceived the world into misjudging the slumbering forces beyond the Elbe. But their day would come. For the time being, like Britain and France, Germany was torn and fatigued from a century of bloody religious wars, and happy to hear the simple gospel of Locke. But shortly thereafter, the earnest doubts of a Scot named Hume would trouble the philosopher from Königsberg far more than anyone in Paris or London.

Locke, as much a child of Descartes as the less influential

but more explicitly rationalistic Malebranche across the Channel, trained the Cartesian *cogito* upon the sensations of experience. He allotted to the labors of reason the modest role of reflecting upon those experiences, ordering them, and arriving at sensible empirical conclusions about them. Since our experience comes from the senses, and the senses only present our physical circumstances, it followed that everyone is going to have different cognitive conditions molding their lives. The stalemate of the religious contest between Christianity and Islam, in the first instance, and between Catholicism and Protestantism, in the second, seemed to underscore the vanity, and even peril, of pursuing any kind of ultimate truth. Tolerance was thus to become one of the watchwords of the enlightened religious ethos. From all this will follow the great 18th-century emphasis on education and legislation as the two ways of conditioning those circumstances, both individually and socially. Thence would hopefully emerge both the happy citizen and the properly ordered state.

Montesquieu inspired the century with the new vision of what legislation can do for human advancement, inaugurating that "science of society" later to be picked up by the sociologists. He inspired them with an enlightened zeal for clarification in making both the laws of nature and the laws of man into the univocal functions of an empirical process. Voltaire's crisp prose and lucid wit charmed a host of cherished beliefs right out of the heads of the upper-crust men of influence, thus eliminating so many obstacles to the ascendancy of the new god of reason. Condorcet would later erect that prospect of progress into a kind of New Jerusalem, but only after a strange priest named Condillac had spread a fully materialistic rendition of Locke's psychology over the face of France. All the while, the popular science of Fontenelle and the *Dictionnaire* of Pierre Bayle were making many suppose that the New Science was on the verge of forcing the question-mark into obsolescence. The sweeping pretenses of the great *Encyclopédie* of Diderot and d'Alembert went on to sustain this illusion with an intimidating literary display.

This same "tidying-up" service to the mind was rendered in the sphere of religion by the new British oracles of deism: Shaftesbury, Toland, and Tindal. The increasing reduction to ethics of both dogma and religion spread from the British Isles and over to the Continent almost as fast as had the new commercial and mercantile spirit. After all, what need had man of God, or God of man, if both had Newton? A single nod of acknowledgement to the Great Architect would suffice for the enlightened deist, and tons of theological and liturgical tomes could be thrown onto the already mounting heap of discarded confusion.

What Montesquieu had done for jurisprudence, Adam Smith did for economics. In this sphere of human activity, too, the acts of man are presented as but factors in a plexus of autonomously functioning economic laws, modeled on the Newtonian laws of motion. To this day, the stock-market report is presented with the same nonchalant resignation as the weather report.

Newton's mechanics had elucidated the universe. Locke's epistemology rendered the same service for human knowledge. Tindal's deism seemed to lay the interminable arguments over religion finally to rest. And Smith laid down the laws of the market. So read the enlightened list of scientific solutions to all man's problems.

But the other lobe of Europe's brain did not idle. Beneath the placid surface of this century, vaunting its candor and open sky of inquiry, men began huddling together as never before in secret societies, and a new network of international design began securing its sequential usurpation of an apparently moribund Catholic Church. Christianity's lingering vigor showed itself, among other things, in the inspiration it left in by far the most redeeming and inspirational product of that otherwise so cerebral century: its music.

Hold up your ear to the year 1729, for example, and you will hear the voice of Voltaire, just back from two years in England, busy outlining his *Lettres Philosophiques*, urging France to debunk its grand heritage and listen to Locke. But stay tuned and you will hear in the background Johann Sebastian Bach's *St. Matthew Passion*, and find yourself in tears of devotion. Move your ear over now to the 1740's and you will hear Lamettrie holding forth vociferously about his materialistic masterpiece, *L'Homme Machine*, but suddenly an interfering sound of English voices from across the Channel intervenes: indeed, King George the Second has just risen, transfixed at a concert, for the Hallelujah Chorus of Handel's *Messiah* has just premiered in London.

All this is only to point out that the Age of Reason was still inhabited by men of flesh and blood, and it is a cheerful tribute to the basic sanity of Europe that in the very age of overpreened rationalism, something deeper lifted itself from within this civilization and gave the world, among many others, Bach, Handel, Haydn, and Mozart.

When, late in the century, the slow maturation of Kant's genius finally peaked in the intimidating bulk of his three *Critiques*, this complex era—full of beautiful music, secret societies, revolutionary politics, and a tangled network of philosophical innovations, all yearning in their own way for a common conceptual denominator—this complex era was at last sifted by the sovereign method we have just examined, and Kant was buried in Königsberg in 1804.

Besides the contrasting musical splendor, there were a few contrasting thinkers, too. One of them was Jean-Jacques Rousseau. His ardent appeal for the purer, wilder forces of nature was hardly appeased by the moral imperative of Kant which it inspired. Indeed, the very form and classical clarity of a Mozart or a Haydn blended too nicely with the staidness of rationalism to be able to serve as an outlet for the primordial furies men like Rousseau sought to vent. Foreshadowed by Rousseau and a host of other factors, the Romantic Movement broke forth from the Kantian critique as a kind of filial rebel, demanding immediate tactile access to the "thing-in-itself," the beloved world, which Kant had neatly sealed off from human view. Schubert's *lieder* sang about it. Byron and Shelly versified it. Beethoven sawed out several of its tonal faces in his later string quartets. And, in what may serve as an emblem of this whole transfiguration, the old legend of the damned Faust was taken up by Goethe and filled with the new fire; the old soul-seller finds salvation at last, for his ceaseless yearning was to be one of the sacraments of the new age.

All this sudden quickening of Teutonic inspiration is an homage to Kant and a revolt at once. He was the one who so tightly circumscribed the legitimate sphere of reason's exercise. Goethe typifies the subsequent reaction in his repeated decrying of Newton. That mathematical slice of reality proffered by the English mechanist is not the world of color, richness and ineffable beauty that the Romantics of the new century longed profoundly to experience and sincerely to express.

More of an homage than a revolt was the other great aftermath of Kant: the German Idealists. We cannot expand here upon the immense speculative importance of their pursuit of the lights of Kant. But it must be said that they do stand to Kant as Spinoza did to Descartes: as the metaphysicians working out the real consequences of the new point of departure. Hegel, especially, never looked back to Newton once his eyes had followed Kant's finger to that solar center of his Copernican revolution. Kant did little more than point to the transcendental ego back behind all our thought. He then returned to Newton and the New Science, confident that he had got them nicely anchored in a new harbor of impregnable calm. Hegel, however, stared with transfixed eyes at that interior, *a priori* subject, and began walking steadily towards that weird sun, all the time with his back to the world. Probably the greatest genius of modern philosophy, Hegel achieves also the purest consummation of the metaphysical message awaiting us at the heart of the *cogito.*

Another dissenting voice in the Enlightenment was that of Johann Herder, who had pointed with insistence at all the complexities and obscurities of human history, and dared the over-confident reason of his day to make a clear, distinct map of all *that.* Of course, Hegel will comply willingly enough, but in a quite different context, and only after abstracting his method from many of those complexities. Herder's challenge struck a different note in the German soul from that of broad metaphysical systematization: it was the call to scholarship.

Turning to that jungle of historical detail and conflicting texts about the past, a new and redoubtable figure rose from the Germanies, and one so unlike a Bach or a Hegel, the manifold resources of this people could no longer be overlooked. Here came the careful, exasperatingly thorough and painstakingly critical hero of the 19th century: the German scholar. No personage or event of history, no manuscript or cuneiform rock-slab, no religious custom, no political institution, no form of currency, husbandry, or global navigation would henceforth veil its secret from the sedulous inquisitions of these new battalions of indefatigable pundits. The whole century will virtually churn with their gathering, editing, translating and collating of the written relics of human history.

We have thus been given a kind of triple legacy from the Kantian critique: 1) a host of Romantic rebels, bent on intense and passionate experience and its spontaneous translation into letters, art and music, holding this to be the true avenue to reality; 2) a trio of brilliant Idealist philosophers—Hegel, Fichte, and Schelling—leaving us with the first attempt ever to map out, as transcendental cartographers, the whole unexplored frontier of human subjectivity, far from, because "prior to," the deterministic scheme of Newton; and (3) a whole throng of newly trained *Gelehrten* (scholars), destined to comb through the words of history, and give us, at the very least, definitive editions of books about those things Kant still permits us to know.

Naturally, the rest of Europe was not sleeping during this explosion of Germanic invention. August Comte, in particular, was to pick up what was left of empiricism after the Kantian revolution. He gave birth to that long, still living, line of positivists, holding strictly to the most rigorous possible examination of phenomena, and the most ascetic abnegation of any further attempts to rescue the now defunct "thing-in-itself." France can boast him. England, with greater warrant, will point to John Stuart Mill.

In a very general way, we can characterize the 19th century under three headings: 1) in philosophy: as the pursuit of a new philosophical foothold capable of standing up to the Kantian critique. The Idealist solution, especially Hegel's, will establish itself as a new permanent possibility for the Western mind, and enjoy see-saw popularity as successive ages wrestle with its many-faceted dialectic. Other, more voluntaristic and existentialist attempts, such as those of Schopenhauer, Nietzsche and Kierkegaard, will evidence the severity of the blow Kant had dealt to modern metaphysical speculation; 2) in scholarship: following the vanguard of such German masters as Friedrich August Wolff and Leopold von Ranke, a host of new Bible critics and philologists, with a new fervor for dissertations and documentation, will pour out thousands of studies, turning especially to the field of history and the newly discovered civilizations of antiquity. Mesopotamia, Egypt, and India will slowly tell their exotic stories to a curious Europe; 3) and in science:

...ah yes, in science: it is here where the real fire of the age is burning.

The Enlightenment dream of getting out that last definitive edition of the *Encyclopédie* was still glowing in many a laboratory. Physics had been the first of the sciences to be mathematicized through the mechanics of Galileo and Newton in the 17th century. Through men like Dalton, Avogadro, and Mendelev, chemistry followed suit in the 19th century. Biology, with its forbidding complexity, was reluctantly and only imperfectly to follow in the 20th, as the intellectual world finally came to a separate peace with the visions of Darwin. But what was conspicuous in all of these 19th century studies was *data:* data on the atom, data on molecules, historical data, psychological data, sociological data, fossil data and so on. The encyclopedias filled up quickly, and the suggestion was made by not a few thinkers that philosophy would have ample work to do if it simply helped out in the ordering of all that data. It would be nice, the harrowed scientist dreamed, if someone would try to get an overview of all these mountains of research and make a kind of map to facilitate its manipulation. Nor would a word or two of interpretation be out of place. Such was the vision of philosophy offered by Herbert Spencer, for example, substantially the same as that to be proposed by the 20th-century thinker, Bertrand Russell.

In a final attempt to sum up the modern mind's progressive disorientation, and to help us to approach Husserl, I shall have to say a word or two about the two great intellectual disciplines in which the triumphant new sciences had put so much faith: logic and mathematics. It is significant that by the end of the 19th century, the combined confusions produced by Positivism, Idealism, and Romanticism, and the approaching crisis in the sciences caused by the slow uncurtaining of the uncanny world of electro-magnetism, brought many thinkers to cling tightly to the two-pronged anchor of logic and mathematics. Or, to invert the metaphor, the immutable rules of the mind and the mathematical scaffolding of the universe seemed like two last mountain summits above the rising flood of revolution, evolution and all the warring theories of the age. But the flood kept rising.

We might note in passing that the man who, more than anyone else, prepared the way for the coming 20th century's growing love-affair with fantasy literature, was a logician and mathematician at once. Before the *Wizard of Oz*, *The Hobbit* and all the others, there was, of course, Alice, *Alice in Wonderland*. This little girl's two escape-routes from reality—the rabbit-hole and the looking-glass—led to only two among hundreds of escapist asylums the coming age would seek. The world was to grow less and less lovable, ever darker and weirder, and the human imagination, deprived of its traditional poetry and innocence, would learn more and more to exercise its own Kantian "spontaneity." The pertinence of these remarks will become clearer when we examine Chesterton's *Orthodoxy*. (See Part III, Chapter 4.)

Thus the researches began, close behind the vanguard of the new German scholars. And new hypotheses about anything and everything followed soon. The words "evolution" and "origin" began to appear in book titles with a tiring frequency, dealing with the origin and evolution of man, of language, of science, of religion, of the state, of our instincts, and of anything else yet outside the parade of progress. Chesterton will have fun chiding some of the latter products of this new obsession in the 20th century. It mattered little what you wrote about, he remarked, for "as long as you begin with a long word like 'evolution' the rest will roll harmlessly past."[27]

As it turns out, men began to ask about the origin and evolution even of logic and mathematics; but as soon as the

27. EM, 24.

thinkers trained in the Cartesian or Kantian mind-set opened their mouths to give what they thought would be a simple and definitive answer, they discovered they had nothing to say. So a number of them did an about-face, rushed back to their data, and tried to find out where we got math and logic from to begin with.

George Boole and Augustus De Morgan in England, and later Gottlob Frege in Germany, claimed that logic hails basically from the same structural clarities as mathematics, and can thus be revamped by a thorough application of algebraic symbols, with the resulting elimination of all traces of rhetoric and grammar. A cognate development occurred in mathematics itself, as Carl Friedrich Gauss, and later Janos Bolyai, Nikolai Lobachevsky and George Riemann discovered the non-Euclidean geometries, showing that one could found a coherent geometry on postulates other than the traditional ones. This led in the coming century to an increasing interest in the so-called axiomatic theories, where the hitherto restricted "point of departure" becomes almost arbitrary; the chosen axioms need only be mutually non-contradictory and independent. Rather than evident principles, they become mere rules of a game. The horrible blow dealt to all of this by Gödel's "incompleteness theorems" in the early 1930's came too late to concern our present narration. It is fun, though, to keep it in mind.

There were, toward the end of the century, various attempts to fashion or find a new platform for philosophy. The burgeoning natural sciences, the probing scholars and indeed the new rise of the "social sciences," all were taking one domain of reality after another off the field of philosophical inquiry and putting them under the scientific methodology of the new sciences.

This finally happened, as already suggested, to those two queens of clarity and certitude themselves. The new science that laid claims on them was psychology, and it was first as an exponent, and then as an opponent of this last reduction, that Edmund Husserl appeared at the turn of the 20th century.

Husserl was quite convinced that modern man had found the scientific tools to manage all the newly discovered powers of nature. He thought the physical universe in particular was being taken forever out of the hands of the philosopher and being put under the ever more exacting scrutiny of the physicist. The inner world of the soul was likewise being successfully claimed by the new psychologists. If philosophy were to survive in this brave new world of pan-scientism, it too would have to mark off its own strictly delimited sphere of inquiry, and fashion its own precision instruments. It was to this task that Edmund Husserl turned his energies.

5. HUSSERL: THE UNIVERSE BRACKETED

Husserl first was drawn to mathematical studies, just like Descartes. The preoccupation with a mathematically stylized clarity will afflict his efforts in philosophy as it did Descartes's. As the crises in mathematics arose, he followed the new solution of reducing the laws of numbers and dimensions to the apparently more fundamental laws of psychology. Thus his first book, *The Philosophy of Arithmetic* (1891), attempted to do just that. The great mathematician-logician Gottlob Frege, however, pointed out to Husserl that he had confused the prerogatives of the subjective and the objective orders, and brought him to see that whatever numbers may be, they are grasped by the mind as an objective *something*. This reversal, together with Franz Brentano's articulate defense of the scholastic doctrine of intentionality, inspired Husserl to seek the true foundations of both logic and mathematics right along the contours of that immediate frontier where object and subject first touch.

The inner states of consciousness and their genesis belong to psychology, and the behavior of the world of things to the physical sciences. But in the very intentional act of the mind in knowing, and the very intentional object which first and originally presents itself to consciousness, Husserl claimed to have found a yet unexplored field. But not just any field, such that it would be one more empirical science besides geology, medicine, or psychology. Upon this newly identified ground, Husserl contended, all the other sciences must needs stand. It was absolutely fundamental. Whatever knowledge one possesses, whatever experiences one has, the primal fact of intentional consciousness and its intended object was presupposed by all, yet examined by none. Here was a new sphere of basic enquiry in need of strict scientific treatment.

At first blush, this hardly seems to be anything new. Was not the introspective grasp of the *cogito* (I think) and the *Ich denke überhaupt* (the fact that I think at all) the new philosophical focus discovered by Descartes and Kant? Husserl conceded this readily. But he pointed to a crucial difference. Descartes had the right intention, but went neither far enough nor proceeded carefully enough. His *cogito* remained on the empirical level, and thus was not yet secured against the encroachment of the empirical sciences. Kant, on the other hand, had failed to appreciate the intrinsic relatedness of the conscious act to the objective content it intuited, thus assigning all formal cognitive structures to the subject. Husserl, however, believed that he had found the key to carry the frustrated effort of both these forerunners to a new and definitive consummation.

In 1900–1901, Husserl's *Logical Investigations* appeared in German, and in them he both brilliantly refuted the psychologism he had earlier adhered to, and began to outline the famous phenomenological method that was to make him famous. To his mind, all philosophers and thinkers use this method to one degree or another, but no one had yet isolated and systematically presented it. That task, he thought, had fallen to him.

In a nutshell, the phenomenological method purports to teach us how to program cognitive innocence. By applying the various "reductions" of this method, Husserl promises to outdo the Cartesian *Meditations* and their methodical doubt. Rather than engaging in such an active and thus presumptuous endeavor as doubt, Husserl asks us only to "withhold" our judgments about whatever we wish to phenomenologically behold. This withholding, or suspension (he often uses the Greek word, *epochē*) of all previous ideas, opinions, prejudices, etc., is designed to free the "thing itself" so that it can show itself to you.

Once it has broken through all those interferences—that is, once you have put them all "in brackets" (in German, *Einklammerung*)—you will be face-to-face with a pure "phenomenon." The next step is to see the phenomenon from as many aspects as possible, so that it may be further purified of all non-essential accidents still adhering to it, and thus be "reduced" to an *eidos* (an idea, or essence). This essence is then intuited, and there you have the underlying basic intentional act intending the basic intentional object—the real foundation for all the empirical knowledge you may have of that object. Husserl hoped that, in this way, every science and art could be phenomenologically underpinned with a "regional ontology," consisting of a science of all the eidetic essences at the basis of all possible empirical findings.

This new nomenclature can be, as with Kant, confusing. Not only do Husserl's epigones use it in varying ways, but the master himself—a perfectionist *par excellence*—was forever overhauling and refining his method. Nonetheless we can easily identify these two basic steps: 1) the historical reduction, designed to bracket all that is subjective, theoretical, or traditional, with the goal of bringing the pure phenomenon to light, that it may show itself as it is to consciousness; and

2) the eidetic reduction, bracketing all adventitious and nonessential details of the phenomenon, with the goal of bringing its pure essence, or *eidos*, to light. To one aspect of this eidetic reduction we will return in a moment. Most of those who call themselves phenomenologists today use, in one variation or another, this double-stepped procedure as an aid to the clear and objective grasp of their objects of inquiry—be they works of art, moral values, social structures, psychological acts, "numinous" phenomena, or whatever. The immense fecundity of the researches in these and other domains forbids us to gainsay Husserl's contribution in the area of scientific methodology.

But there is more. It is no secret that around 1913, as if Husserl had suddenly revealed to his circle of pupils that he was really a black magician in disguise, almost all of them abandoned him, and for good. As they walked off, they still had their volumes of *The Logical Investigations* under their arms, but another book he had just shown them was left at the feet of their deeply disappointed teacher: *The Ideas for a Pure Phenomenology.* This book disclosed a new and fateful step in Husserl's method, and most of his adherents held it to be a step over a precipice. Husserl had become an idealist.

It is extremely significant that this last great epistemological innovator ended up adamantly maintaining that our consciousness *of* a world necessarily preceded our consciousness *in* a world. It is somewhat ill-boding that the man who wished to perfect the work begun by Descartes and Kant spent the last twenty-five years of his life refining a method which he was convinced must lead to the denial of any truly robust existence of a world beyond consciousness. Not a little of his subsequent work will be an earnest but unavailing effort to convince us that he is not a solipsist, as in the *Méditations Cartésiennes* of 1929.

I do not intend to enter into an analysis of his idealistic phase here. Those who still use the earlier steps of his method are careful to distinguish their applications from his later version of the same. Nor do I wish to discuss the comparative value of the phenomenological method in all its possible philosophical and scientific usages. Several distinctions and cautions should be urged. For our purposes, however, only one feature of the method is relevant, and it is not in his infamous third, transcendental reduction, where he attempts to reduce the eidetic intuition itself to a transcendental consciousness as a finally irreducible phenomenological residue. The serious consequences of all this should be evident enough to any unsleeping realist. The first seed of Husserl's plunge into idealism is not, however, in step three, in the transcendental reduction, but in step two, and in the attitude of mind fostered in the ostensibly "safe" procedure of the eidetic reduction.

When Husserl is working away at the phenomenon and "bracketing" all the unessentials, there is one "unessential" that is chaperoned into the brackets, not with the civility and politeness of a gentleman, but rather with the iron coaxing of a crow-bar. For with a disarming matter-of-factness, Husserl has asked us to shove something in between those narrow brackets that no sane man would even remotely associate with parentheses: the whole expanse of the universe!

Again, our philosopher attempts to pacify us. Bracketing the universe does not mean that it is not there, he assures us. Husserl, like Descartes, is quite sure that the cosmos is out there. "I am conscious of a world,"[28] he insists. He ascertains that around his conscious act lies "an empty mist of dark indetermination [which] populates itself with graphic possibilities or suspicions, and only the 'form' of the world, precisely as 'world', is traced out. The indeterminate sur-

28. *Ideen zu einer reinen Phänomenologie und phänomenologischen Philosophie, erstes Buch*, "Allgemeine Einführung in die reine Phänomenologie," §§27–32 (The Hague: Koehler Verlag, 1976), 56 [my translation].

roundings is furthermore infinite. The misty and never fully determinable horizon is necessarily there."[29] Now already in his earlier presentation of the phenomenological method, we had been asked to bracket the actual existence of the object under consideration, as it does not enter into an essential intuition. Here in the *Ideas*, with all the emphasis one could desire, this dispensability of existence is extended to the entire creation.

The "mistiness" of the world is obviously a disqualification for a Cartesian mind. "For us who approach the gate of phenomenology . . . we require only a few of the very general characteristics of the natural standpoint [*die natürliche Einstellung*], which in our descriptions have already emerged with a sufficient fullness of clarity. *It was precisely this fullness of clarity that was our special concern*."[30] [emphasis added]

He looks up from his desk at the world and repeats: "I find constantly present as my *vis-à-vis* a spatio-temporal reality, to which I myself belong. . . ." This ingredient in the "natural standpoint" he calls its "general thesis" (*Generalthesis*), i.e., the world is *posited* by everyone as being there. Husserl is an honest man, and realizes the world's reality does lay a certain claim on his attention. But, apparently satisfied that, by granting it the high status of a "general thesis," he has duly honored that claim, he turns around and utters these remarkable words: "Now instead of remaining in this standpoint, we shall radically alter it. It is now imperative [*es gilt jetzt*] that we convince ourselves of the principial possibility of this alteration."[31] I should think so!

Husserl tries to palliate the inevitable ring of absurdity in these pages by shifting his vocabulary around so much, you

29. Ibid., 57.
30. Ibid., 61.
31. Ibid.

hardly have time to channel your indignation towards any one word. For instance, after using the image of the brackets, he assures us that what he really means is simply that he is placing the general thesis "out of action" [*außer Aktion*], but that it somehow still is "there for us, and will forever remain there as conscious 'reality' [*Wirklichkeit*], even if we choose to bracket it." If that has not yet soothed us, he tries again:

> I do not deny this "world," as if I were a sophist; I do not doubt its existence, as if I were a skeptic; but I do practice the "phenomenological" *epochē*, which completely blocks off to me any judgment about spacio-temporal existence.[32]

All this continues for tens of pages, but the only litmus test I apply to the text is, to ask a variation on the question Christ once put to his Apostles: "What do you say that the world is?" This is his answer:

> [T]he entire spatiotemporal world, to which man and the human ego reckon themselves as subordinate individual realities, has, according to its *meaning*, only intentional being—one that has only a secondary, relative meaning of being. It is a being [*ein Sein*], that consciousness [*das Bewusstsein*] posits in its experiences, that is principally only intuitable and determinable as an identity of motivated manifolds of phenomena [*Identisches von motivierten Erscheinungsmannigfaltigkeiten*]—but *beyond this it is nothing* [*ein Nichts*].[33] [emphasis added at end]

CONCLUSION TO PART II

Chesterton once commented on Descartes's original attempt to begin anew the business of thought. This will serve as our

32. Ibid., 65.
33. Ibid., 106.

concluding characterization of the peculiar agitation of mind the new critical spirit bred:

> I do not deny that it is sometimes a good thing to empty the mind of the mere accumulation of secondary and tertiary impressions. If what is meant is something which a friend of mine once called "a mental spring clean," then I can see what it means. But the most drastic spring clean in a house does not generally wash away the house. It does not tear down the roof like a cobweb, or pluck up the walls like weeds.... And the true formula is not so much to empty the mind as to discover that we cannot empty the mind, by emptying it is as much as we can. In other words, we always come back to certain fundamentals which are convictions, because we can hardly even conceive their contraries. But it is the paradox of human language that though these truths are, in a manner past all parallel, hard and clear, yet any attempt to talk about them always has the appearance of being hazy and elusive.[34]

This "hazy and elusive" character of our initial attempts to "talk about" the first salute of the universe is one of the most essential matters to grasp about human knowledge. Our next chapter will attempt to draw out the various lessons, guided by Chesterton's *Orthodoxy*. But we can affirm now that Chesterton stands very much on the side of Aristotle, who maintains in his *Physics* that there is only one way to pursue the principles of reality:

> The natural way of doing this is to start from the things which are more knowable and obvious to us and proceed towards those which are clearer and more knowable by nature....[35]

So far, one could imagine Descartes nodding his head approvingly, although the use of the words "knowable and

34. FF, 43.
35. Aristotle, *Physics*, I, 1, 184 a 17–21.

obvious" instead of the Cartesian pair of "clear and distinct" portends a falling out. The next lines of Aristotle confirm this suspicion:

> Now what is plain and obvious at first is rather *confused masses*, the elements and principles of which become known to us later by analysis. Thus we must advance from generalities to particulars; for it is a whole that is best known to sense perception, and a generality is a kind of whole, comprehending many things within it, like parts.[36] [emphasis added]

Aristotle wrote elsewhere that in any discourse "our discussion will be adequate if it has *as much clearness as the subject-matter admits of, for precision is not to be sought for alike in all discussions*."[37] [emphasis added] If the subject-matter is the world itself, how precise can our first encounter with it be? To this question, both Aristotle and Descartes deliver the same answer: not very precise at all. The difference is that Descartes, and after him a host of modern philosophers, refuse to have anything to do with such an imprecise principle. Aristotle realistically replies that we will have to make do with it, because it is the only principle we have got. For him, the indistinct world *is* the point of departure of philosophy. If you start anywhere else, or with anything else, you stop philosophizing. Many a modern philosopher typically tries to begin with precision, but often enough fails to precisely follow the full implications of such an outset. Again, Chesterton:

> To almost all the modern moral and metaphysical systems, as stated by the moderns themselves, I should be content to add the comment, 'Mate in three moves.' That is, these thinkers have landed themselves in positions which are already doomed by the laws of thought; or, to change the

36. Ibid., a22–26.
37. *Nichomachean Ethics*, I, 3 1094 a 12–14.

> mathematical to the military figure, their positions are outflanked, their communications cut and their ammunition very obviously running short. In many cases, their form of revolt is one that can only be a sort of temporary formation.[38]

There is a standard complaint against Thomists, and like-minded realists, that they just slam down their fists on the table and try to settle the question about the world's existence by violence. With all deference to Etienne Gilson's masterful defense of a "methodical" and yet non-critical realism, I, for one, should like also to celebrate the brute eloquence of the fist. As Gilson himself says at the beginning of his remarkable book, *Thomist Realism and the Critique of Knowledge*, the basic problem of trying to prove the world's existence is that "the very principles which make such a demonstration necessary, at the same time render the attempted proof impossible."[39] St. Augustine said that having God and something else is less than having God alone. We might expand upon this and say that accepting the evidence of the world's existence plus an argument would be less convincing than the evidence alone.

An anecdote about Samuel Johnson is often cited in this context. It is well known, but a closer look at it will, I think, drive the point home. Johnson's biographer recounts:

> After we came out of the church, we stood talking for some time together of Bishop Berkeley's ingenious sophistry to prove the non-existence of matter, and that everything in the universe is merely ideal. I observed that though we are satisfied his doctrine is not true, it is impossible to refute it. I never shall forget the alacrity with which Johnson

38. CM, 197.

39. Etienne Gilson, *Thomist Realism and the Critique of Knowledge* (San Francisco: Ignatius Press, 1986).

> answered, striking his foot with mighty force against a large stone, till he rebounded from it. "I refute it thus."[40]

The immense instructive value of this paragraph lies not in the "cleverness" of Johnson's reply—as if he had merely raised his eyebrows with a twinkle in the eye and let some choice words roll over his tongue. No, the whole force of this oft-quoted incident lies in the sheer lionesque energy of the instant, full-bodied retort. The "alacrity with which he answered," hurling his whole heavy bulk into a kick of the nearest, hardest THING he could find—in this case, a rock—a kick so total, so transrational, so almost astrophysical, the big man rebounds from it as if the rock had reared up and whacked the good doctor right back. And of course, the whole point is that it did; Johnson had intentionally provoked it.

In a letter to his fiancée just before the turn of the century, Chesterton offered his whole message in a little parable:

> A cosmos one day being rebuked by a pessimist replied: "How can you who revile me consent to speak by my machinery? Permit me to reduce you to nothingness and then we will discuss the matter." Moral: You should not look a gift universe in the mouth.[41]

40. *Boswell's Life of Johnson*, ed. by A. and I. Ehrenpreis (New York, 1955), 127–28.

41. Maisie Ward, *Gilbert Keith Chesterton*, 65.

III

The First Salute of the Universe

There is at the back of all our lives an abyss of light, more blinding and unfathomable than any abyss of darkness; and it is the abyss of actuality, of existence, of the fact that things truly are, and that we ourselves are incredibly and sometimes incredulously real. It is the fundamental fact of being, as against not being; it is unthinkable, yet we cannot unthink it, though we may sometimes be unthinking about it; unthinking and especially unthanking. For he who has realized this reality knows that it does outweigh, literally to infinity, all lesser regrets or arguments for negation, and that under all our grumblings there is a subconscious substance of gratitude.

~ G.K.C., *Chaucer*[1]

INTRODUCTION

Descartes, Kant, and Husserl, rejecting the evident imprecision of the common man's world, set off in search of a precise evidence upon which that shaky world itself could be steadied. But in doing so, they disregarded their own saner instincts, and made the modern philosopher only too often into a remote and esoteric specialist. As we turn to Chesterton's philosophical debut, it is gratifying to be able to invoke

1. C, 161.

one very exceptional German philosopher—one who found his way through the more abstruse speculative craftsmen of his ken, and scaled the European mental mountaintop known as Thomas Aquinas. Returning then to his mother tongue, this philosopher showed what sweetness and light that marvelous language can generate, once its communion with the Latin sources of Western reason is restored.

The philosopher I refer to is Josef Pieper. In 1957 Professor Pieper delivered a radio talk entitled "What do we mean by the 'Christian West'?"[2] In this clear and illuminating address, the speaker asks us what it is that constitutes the essential ingredient in Western, Christian thought. He concludes that it can be summarized in three words: theologically established worldliness (*theologisch gegründete Weltlichkeit*). In the West alone, theology has served to buttress the claims of finite reality. Elsewhere, it usually does the opposite. In these three words, we find the bridge between the "unworldly" cogitations of our three modern innovators, straying ever closer to the acosmic tendencies their principles imply, and the very "worldly" legacy of authentic Western thought.

The characteristic Occidental tenor of mind is braced in Aristotle's defense of the proper reality of finite substances, and the immanent activities they put forth. It is then crowned by the metaphysical discovery, intellectually irrigated by Christian revelation, that God created this very real world out of nothing at all. For us—creatures among creatures—that world is necessarily the first object of our pondering. One could even say that Biblical revelation not only revealed God, but that it also revealed the world. Once reassured of its native object (created material reality), reason would take off on its own—indeed only too often in ungrateful antagonism to the faith that had vindicated its

2. "Was heisst 'Christliche Abendland'?" in *Tradition als Herausforderung* (Munich: Koesel, 1963), 36–47; quote, 39.

rights. Rash interpretation of modern science is only too often a case in point.

The dogma of the Incarnation may seem far afield from physics, but, as Stanley Jaki has asserted: "the fact, the great historical fact, still to be set forth in all its details and turned into cultural consciousness, is that science owes its very birth to that dogma." Indeed, he goes on to identity "the only viable birth of science [to be] in terms of the Christian belief in creation and Incarnation."[3] Chesterton's *Orthodoxy* goes a long way toward justifying this claim. And it does so by showing the traditional, pre-Cartesian thinker of the West to be a better, more factual philosopher, precisely because his faith has situated his thought in the very real universe in which the Christian drama occurs. That God-created cosmos is, for the Christian, one big and doggedly insistent fact. So the world into which he gazes as a philosopher, he knows to be all the more solid, all the more worthy of reflection, and all the more transparent to the transcendent, for the simple reason that God Himself has set foot upon it.

1. THE BOOK *ORTHODOXY*

It is commonly held that Chesterton's *Orthodoxy*, certainly the most familiar and popular of his non-fiction works, is a book about Christian apologetics. Despite first-blush appearances, this is not quite true. The book is really about philosophy. It is not a book of systematic philosophy, to be sure. But it is about philosophy. The publishers of a series of religious books included this little volume in its collection, and, with innocent intentions, printed an excerpt from it as

3. Stanley Jaki, acceptance address upon reception of Templeton Prize, London, May, 1987, in *The Wanderer*, Oct. 22, 1987, 83.

blurb on the back cover in greatly enlarged type: "I WISH TO SET FORTH MY FAITH...," followed by the rest of the excerpted paragraph in small type. I wonder if anyone of philosophical propensities is going to bother to read the rest of the paragraph, having been thus bluntly forewarned that theology is in the offing.

As it turns out, the rest of the paragraph—and even the rest of this first sentence—are far more pivotal in bearing upon the subject of *Orthodoxy* than these seven trumpeted syllables. True, Chesterton wishes to set forth his faith, but he wishes to set it forth "*as* [permit me now to emphasize!] *particularly answering the double spiritual need, the need for that mixture of the familiar and the unfamiliar which Christendom has rightly named romance*."[4] A little further on he elaborates: "We need so to view the world as to combine an idea of wonder and an idea of welcome. We need to be happy in this wonderland without being merely comfortable. It is *this* achievement of my creed [Chesterton's emphasis this time!] that I shall chiefly pursue in these pages."

It is *this* achievement of his creed, as satisfying that double spiritual need, of which this book treats. Here is his focus. Now the fact that after wavering both sides of dead center, from blur to blur, the clearly resolved picture turns out to be a glowing portrait of Christianity, surprised no one more than Chesterton himself. That is really the whole point of the book. And we who read the book, miss the point of the book, if we fail to share that surprise. However, we can only prime ourselves for such a surprise by beginning the book with something other than the faith. So rather than with the creed, Chesterton begins with a presentation of his "cosmic theory," intending to "state the philosophy in which I have

4. For this third part of the book, the numerous quotes from *Orthodoxy* will always be taken from the chapter of the book under discussion, but without page numbers. Other works will be footnoted as usual.

come to believe," dealing thereby with "the main problem of this book."

The main problem, at least for modern philosophers, is the problem of where thought begins. That the book obviously and energetically deals just as much with where thought leads to, nonetheless presupposes his point of departure. It is only of interest to him insofar as it hails from precisely that origin. As we have already seen, that origin is the stance of mind to which Chesterton had mentally journeyed as a young man. That he almost lost his way led him close to madness. He writes in the second chapter of the present book: "The man who begins to think without the proper first principles goes mad; he begins to think at the wrong end. And for the rest of these pages we have to try and discover what is the right end."

Chesterton writes in a short preface that the book is "arranged upon the positive principle of a riddle and its answer. It deals with the writer's own solitary and sincere speculations and then with all the startling style in which they were all suddenly satisfied by the Christian Theology." His personal "speculations" that generated this riddle are but the reflectively articulated map of the early crisis of his mind. That crisis, in turn, articulates the luring invitation to walk down the road paved with Cartesian doubts and Kantian critiques.

Before reading the book, one might be tempted to expect of Chesterton a "theologized" philosophy, somewhat after the manner of Maurice Blondel. For Blondel, we recall, philosophy fulfills its highest office in clearly articulating the riddles of man's life and situation, which then can only be satisfactorily answered by dove-tailed doctrines revealed by the Church. Thus, for Blondel, to clarify the philosophical enigma of God, the faith presents the dogma of the Trinity; for the philosophical enigma of guilt, the Redemption; for the enigma of human destiny, the beatific vision, and so on.

Blondel judges the most evolved and perfect philosophy to be the one which has most clearly traced the outlines of its own inadequacy, like so many multiple-shaped holes, each crying out for the conversely contoured dogma that alone can fill it.[5]

Blondel's thought is serious and well worth pondering. But is this what Chesterton is suggesting in his philosophical riddles and their answers in the Christian faith? Though he does use similar words, his intention is quite distinct from that of Blondel. Seeing this difference means understanding one of the most fundamental features of the Western intellectual tradition our author is espousing. But let us follow the gradual unfolding of his thought and see if it helps us to share that sense of surprise which so profoundly inspired his vision.

In 1905 Chesterton had published a work entitled *Heretics*, in which he had exposed the illogicalities of such turn-of-the-century "heretics" as Bernard Shaw, H. G. Wells and Rudyard Kipling. Having been publicly chided for not expounding his own cosmic theory and stating what *he* regards to be true orthodoxy, he replied with the appropriately entitled volume.

Not even attempting a thorough defense of his faith, he chooses "one path of argument." That path, however, turns out to be precisely the philosophical issue of first principles, and how they are secured, defended and finally, surprisingly, nourished and crowned by the Christian faith. It is of enormous importance to his train of thought that these principles are seen as being of a piece with the mental coordinates of Western man. It is the Occidental who is conspicuous for his gusto for an active and imaginative life. In the texts quoted above, the union of "welcome and wonder" is taken

5. Maurice Blondel, *Le problème de la philosophie catholique* (Paris, 1932).

to be a native aspiration of the Western man in the street. That this aspiration can be lost or stifled, Chesterton knows only too well.

Certain alleged tenets of Eastern metaphysics popularized in his day seemed to stylize this loss into a philosophical principle. The modern drift of philosophical thought will be evaluated by Chesterton as a drift away from our home in the West. Repeating in Chapter 1 the story of the man who has to travel far from home in order to finally and truly get there, Chesterton stands up humbly and confesses that he himself is that man. He is the fool who had to go through such "elephantine adventures in pursuit of the obvious."

Our author grew up in a Unitarian household in Victorian England, but was still surrounded by Christian allusions and symbols, and certainly knew the basic doctrines of Christianity as a boy. This has caused some to wonder how he could honestly maintain he had "thought it up for himself." In answering this question, we appreciate the uniqueness of *Orthodoxy*, for it was not Christianity itself that he discovered, but rather its correspondence to common-sense certitudes.

He was not raising his head from the shadows to finally behold the objects standing in the sun. If this were his accomplishment, he would indeed be of the stamp of Blondel. But he is not. He found no holes or shadows in nature, no mere yearnings and frustrated dynamisms, but instead solid things and causal acts. The questions of life were not just answered; they were transfigured. Chesterton saw that it was common sense alone that posited the kind of world every one experiences, and that Christianity alone among religions addressed that world as it is. The faith did answer questions, obviously, but the uncanny thing about it was that it also asked them, just like Christ on the Cross. Questions are a part of reality. And they cry out not only to be answered, but even more to be properly put. The Christian faith rings true for Chesterton because it chimes in with this particular feature of the world, which also rings true.

In other words, common sense does not posit enigmas that long for resolution; but neither does it lay down resolutions that eliminate enigmas. Rather, it lays down the certitude that mysteries are real, and discovers that Christianity is also quite sure of its mysteries. Chesterton will observe "how the flowers of the field or the pains of youth came together in a certain order to produce a certain conviction of Christian orthodoxy. . . ." More than anything else, grace lifted up the yearnings and questions of the natural order and pointed them toward something that even grace itself did not yet bring: glory. But we are already getting ahead of ourselves.

Chapters 2 and 3 Chesterton characterizes as a "preliminary negative sketch." Before proceeding to the treatment of the principles he had discovered, he first exposes two dead-ends in the business of beginning human thought. The first is the attempt to reason one's way to the principles of thought. This, Chesterton maintains, leads to madness if it is pursued all the way through. The second, more than an attempt, is rather a temptation—the temptation of doubting that there can be any principles at all. This leads, while not to madness, nonetheless directly to an equally destructive state of mind: skepticism. Let us examine each danger in turn.

2. THE MANIAC

The first pitfall in discerning principles is dealt with in a chapter whose title[6] reminds us of the chapter "How to be a Lunatic" in the *Autobiography*, which described Chesterton's adolescent struggles over principles. The two chapters are

6. The subheads for the rest of Part III simply reproduce those of *Orthodoxy*.

complementary. In *Orthodoxy*, Chesterton backs off from the historical setting of his early 1890's crisis and tries to delineate a general lesson for the mental consolidation of men at large. The interconnectedness of the speculative and moral principles, highlighted before, is evidenced by the inaugural example he gives. Casting about for a universally dread evil, he would like to turn to sin. It was with this that the "ancient masters" began, with a "fact as practical as potatoes, as plain as a pikestaff." "The strongest saints and the strongest skeptics alike took positive evil as the starting point of their argument." But to modern man, unfortunately, the plainness is gone. In addressing him, we must find an example closer to his spontaneous mental allusions. So Chesterton turns to the other side of the coin: men may quarrel today over whether or not you can lose your soul in the moral order, but few will deny that you can lose your wits in the mental order. Whether or not any of us are sinful, quite a number of us are obviously crazy. As a good rhetorician, realizing that the specimen of a sinner will say little to his contemporary audience, our author trots out a human type still generally judged to be out of order: the madman. "Let us begin, then, with the mad-house; from this evil and fantastic inn let us set forth on our intellectual journey."

The paradoxical turn in this second chapter is that as we await Chesterton's revelation of the antidote that will heal our madness and restore us to the sanity of first principles, we are in for a surprise. It turns out that his diagnosis of the madman's derangement is that it results from an overdose of the very prescription we should expect to have brought his recovery. And what is more, the remedy he *does* prescribe for the cure is precisely what we would commonly consider to be the toxin. For Chesterton asserts that it is *reason* that has wrecked him; and only poetry can put him right. "What peril of morbidity there is for man comes rather from his reason than his imagination."

In order to bar a lurking misunderstanding, we are cautioned that the madman is not already poetic merely by being weird. Quite the contrary, he is banal and tedious to himself, for the "oddities" with which his life abounds "only strike ordinary people," among whom he, by definition, does not number. Indeed, his real problem is that he has next to no poetry in himself at all.

> Poetry is sane because it floats easily in an infinite sea; reason seeks to cross the infinite sea, and so make it finite. The result is mental exhaustion. . . . To accept everything is an exercise, to understand everything a strain. The poet only desires exaltation and expansion, a world to stretch himself in. The poet only asks to get his head into the heavens. It is the logician who seeks to get the heavens into his head.

There is indeed in human knowledge a sea to swim in, a world to stretch in, and a sky to stretch toward. The madman's mania lies in wanting to commandeer these cognitive initiations, casting off the awe and submission of a neophyte and grasping eagerly for the instruments of an experienced engineer. He wants to cross the sea, map out the world, and supervise the sky. And in the process, he feverishly overlooks them all, and goes mad. Logic has gotten fatally mixed into acts for which it was never designed.

> Now speaking quite externally and empirically, we may say that the strongest and most unmistakable mark of madness is this combination between a logical completeness and a spiritual contraction. The lunatic's theory explains a large number of things, but it does not explain them in a large way.

In a word, "the madman is not the man who has lost his reason. The madman is the man who has lost everything except his reason." Chesterton's generalizations may bother minds not accustomed to working with genera. Here, as so often in his writings, he eyes a general truth about most people who "go mad," and bothers little with the details and distinctions a psychiatrist might urge. This particular generalization has, however, born up well under a professional psychiatrist's scrutiny.[7]

The maniac has come to refuse the obvious intellectual exigencies of the world in its flurry of first lessons—what we term "common sense"—and has rushed headlong into a cramped and unhappy pursuit of compensatory logic. And "in many ways the mind moves all the quicker for not being delayed by the things that go with good judgment. He is not hampered by a sense of humor or by charity, or by the dumb certainties of experience."

Chesterton's long analysis of the madman would be of *only* psychiatric interest were it not for the fact that the madman exhibits a quality of mind sometimes found in leading modern philosophers. It is just that the philosopher is usually less honest, or even less logical, than the resolute madman, and thus succeeds in keeping his head on. But the principles in that head are still pointing, Chesterton insists, straight for the madhouse. Something elsewhere in the philosopher's make-up keeps him clear of that unhappy consummation.

We saw how Descartes and Kant still *willed* to affirm extra-mental reality, which caused them to proceed in a way untrue to their own principles, engineering at last a *deus ex machina* to keep the world from vanishing. Hegel bid goodbye to the expediencies, and hurried the principles along to their Idealistic appointments. Husserl merely tried again, after the revolutions in the exact sciences had made Hegel's

7. See John D. Coates, *Chesterton and the Edwardian Cultural Crisis* (London: Hull University Press, 1984), 210–34. We might add Jacques Maritain's remark that "if there is an insane asylum among the pure spirits in heaven, it is only there that we can see Kant's Pure Reason in operation," in *The Peasant of the Garrone* (New York: Macmillan, 1969), 113.

system look a bit pale, and, to his credit, excogitated a purer and more consistent Idealism than even Hegel had done.

Now Hegel and Husserl, you may point out, did not go mad. No, they did not, if you mean they did not foam at the mouth and throw chairs through windows. But there is a quiet madness, too, and I think it is of this sort that Chesterton writes. In a way, the raving bedlamite is still a realist. He believes in hard chairs and breakable windows. Our Idealist sits placidly in the chair and looks out the window, for he and the chair and the window are but aspects of Mind looking at itself. And we shouldn't forget that one of the fundamental features of genuine psychiatric disorder is precisely this sort of severance of contact with reality.

Chesterton will later comment on this again in his book on St. Thomas Aquinas. Just as the madman has somehow disjointed himself from first principles, and as a result sees the world in a different way from the general run of men, the modern philosopher characteristically does the same. "Since the modern world began in the 16th century, nobody's system of philosophy has really corresponded to everybody's sense of reality; to what, if left to themselves, common men would call common sense." The main point here is that the logic is often enough accurate, even complete, but that the point of departure is all wrong. "The modern philosopher claims, like a sort of confidence man, that if once we will grant him this, the rest will be easy; he will straighten out the world, if once he is allowed to give this one twist to the mind."[8]

Our author's descriptions of this maddening self-imprisonment of the mind portray the affliction so pointedly, we may soon recognize some people of our own acquaintance, possibly even ourselves. How often in fact do we find

8. TA, 145.

> . . .this combination between a logical completeness and a spiritual contraction. . . .
>
> . . .a horrible clarity of detail . . . but not hampered by a sense of humor or charity, or by the dumb certainties of experience.
>
> [people living] in the clean and well-lit prison of one idea; . . . sharpened to one painful point . . . without healthy hesitation and healthy complexity.
>
> . . .the combination of an expansive and exhaustive reason with a contracted common sense.

An unexpected result of this rootless reason is the pallor and featurelessness of the world it discloses. In Chesterton's day, the materialist illustrated this best of all: "He understands everything, and everything does not seem worth understanding. . . . If the cosmos of the materialist is the real cosmos, it is not much of a cosmos."

Already in these pages Chesterton turns to the inextricable concomitant of the issue of mind and truth, which is the issue of will and the good. He had decided not to begin with it, but knew that the issues would gravitate back to it in any case. The hypertrophy of reason in the madman and the typically modern thinker not only constricts the universe to a rationalistic chain of arguments, but, with equal dispatch, links it as well to a matching deterministic chain of causes. Both chains are prison chains. The same graying of a gay world results from the latter as from the former.

> [W]hen materialism leads men to complete fatalism (as it generally does), it is quite idle to pretend that it is in any sense a liberating force. It is absurd to say that you are especially advancing freedom when you only use free thought to destroy all free thought. The determinist comes to bind, not to loose.

This persistent interweaving of the theoretical and the practical in the realm of principle becomes a dominant feature in Chesterton's thought. The problem with the impractical person, he will later insist, is not that he is too theoretical, but that he is not theoretical enough. He has not yet *seen* what he has to *do*. His theory never lights up because it is never plugged in to first principles. Like a Christmas tree beautifully strung with halos of colored bulbs, it remains dull and gray because no one bothered to make sure the cord could reach the electric socket. If a theory is truly rooted in those principial energies, it will be a lamp to the feet and a light to the path of the most abstract theoretician.

The maniac's self-contraction is well imaged by the familiar Eastern symbol of the ouroboros, the serpent eating its tail (a symbol curiously dear to many modern mystics and skeptics). This is the first explicit mention of the "cyclical" East in *Orthodoxy*, and we shall see how this specter of serpentine self-consumption seems to haunt the mind of Chesterton throughout this and subsequent books. As Chapter 2 approaches its end, the argument swells with a typical crescendo of conviction, presenting to the imagination two great symbols for the two principal belligerents in the war over human thought: one is the reptilian ring, simplified as the Circle. The other is the Cross.

The Circle represents the incarcerating habit of mind we have been exploring. It is the maniac's "reason used without root, reason in the void." Starting the wheels to turn without checking the brakes, and with little experience in managing the wheel, the vehicle of thought begins to spin around itself like a car on ice. We are reminded of the strange legend of the oley-oley bird, the one that flies in circles of diminishing diameter, until it has vanished like a star down a black hole. Only the angularity of a cruciform interruption can break the spell of such a swirl.

> A man cannot think himself out of mental evil; for it is actually the organ of thought that has become diseased, ungovernable, and, as it were, independent. He can only

> be saved by will or faith. The moment his mere reason moves, it moves in the old circular rut; he will go round and round his logical circle. . . . Decision is the whole business here; a door must be shut forever. Every remedy is a desperate remedy. Every cure is a miraculous cure. Curing a madman is not arguing with a philosopher; it is casting out a devil.

The error is not in the reason but in the root of reason, or rather in the lack thereof. The "insanity is proved not by any error in their argument, but by the manifest mistake of their whole lives." Something must *happen* to such a man. The circle must be broken. What is it then that makes men sane? Chesterton promises to make that clear by the end of the book. But he does already give it a name—he calls it "mysticism." We need not be overly pedantic in insisting that Chesterton does not have in mind "the supernatural state of soul in which God is known in a way that no human effort or exertion could ever succeed in producing,"[9] or any of the blurrier notions a less disciplined 20th-century mind might volunteer. But the word was not poorly chosen.

> Mysticism keeps men sane. As long as you have mystery you have health; when you destroy mystery you create morbidity. The ordinary man has always been sane because the ordinary man has always been a mystic. He has permitted the twilight. He has always had one foot in earth and the other in fairyland.

For Chesterton, the common man's initial response to the universe is the response to a mystery. The mystic here is the man who has "cared more for truth than for consistency," whose "spiritual sight is stereoscopic," able to hold on to even apparently contradictory messages from the world,

9. John A. Hardon, *Modern Catholic Dictionary* (New York: Doubleday, 1980), 367.

"seeing two different pictures at once and yet seeing all the better for that." The sane man, the "mystic," is so humbled by the immense mystery of the cosmos, he would not dream of trying definitively to understand it. It just does not seem like the kind of thing to do with a universe. The cosmos as a whole obviously presents itself to us as something *given*, and not as a problem or a theorem; it is a datum. It is precisely here, in this "mystical" vision of the universe that our cognitive life really began. In Chesterton's first book of essays he spoke of this beginning, though he did at that time use the word "mysticism" in its more restricted sense:

> The most unfathomable schools and sages have never attained to the gravity which dwells in the eyes of a baby three months old. It is the gravity of astonishment at the universe, and astonishment at the universe is not mysticism, but a transcendent common sense.[10]

That there finally is a continuity between this first "mysticism," this "transcendent common sense" of the vision of the creation, and the ultimate mysticism of the vision of the Creator, is one of the deepest lessons of the Christian tradition. It is perhaps the favorite lesson of Chesterton, returned to in many of his later books.

> I think there is a mystical minimum in human history and experience, which is at once too obscure to be explained and too obvious to be explained away.[11]
>
> This simple sense of wonder at the shapes of things, and at their exuberant independence of our intellectual standards and our trivial definitions, is the basis of spirituality. . . .[12]
>
> The more we attempt to analyze that strange element of wonder, which is the soul of all the arts, the more we shall

10. DE, 149.
11. UD, 13.
12. DE, 70.

see that it must depend on some subordination of self to a glory existing beyond it, and even in spite of it.[13]

The round, moon-like face, the round moon-like spectacles of Samuel Pickwick move through the tale [Dickens's *Pickwick Papers*] as emblems of a certain spherical simplicity. They are fixed in that grave surprise that may be seen in babies; that grave surprise which is the only real happiness that is possible to man.[14]

The mystery of life is the plainest part of it. [emphasis added] The clouds are curtains of darkness, the confounding vapors; these are the daily weather of the world.[15]

The poor maniac, along with many a modern philosopher, unnaturally overlooks the universe and ironically throws himself into a tizzy trying to figure it out. Refusing to submit to any mystery, he excogitates inquisitive ruts deeper and deeper into his own mind. In *Heretics*, to which *Orthodoxy* is a sequel, Chesterton wrote of the maniac: "He may turn over and explore a million objects, but he must not find that strange object, the universe; for if he does he will have a religion, and be lost."[16] Scanning the universe frantically with the searchlight of reason, he paradoxically overlooks the whole thing. Along this same axis of thought lie Chesterton's frequent burlesques of one of his favorite modern butts: the tourist.

The globe-trotter lives in a smaller world than the peasant. He is always breathing an air of locality. London is a place, to be compared to Chicago; Chicago is a place, to be compared with Timbuktu. But Timbuktu is not a place, since there, at least, live men who regard it as the universe and breathe, not an air of locality, but the winds of the world.

The more dead and dry and dusty a thing is the more it

13. II, 213.
14. CD, 95.
15. WB, 131–32.
16. H, 13.

> travels about; dust is like this and the thistle-down.... Fertile things are somewhat heavier, like the heavy fruit trees on the pregnant mud of the Nile.[17]

One must stay put somewhere, anywhere, in order to settle down into an authentically human posture, and take in the universe at a glance. "The moment we are rooted in a place, the place vanishes. We live like a tree with the whole strength of the universe."[18]

Chesterton's point here is that only by holding on jealously to that first wide-eyed wonder of our tender days, when we first accosted the world, can we keep our balance in the face of that world's subsequent epistemological challenges. It is a kind of fidelity. In his later book on Aquinas, our author speaks in this context of the Angelic Doctor being "faithful to his first love," for "he immediately recognized a real quality in things; and afterwards resisted all the disintegrating doubts arising from the nature of those things."[19] Tempered by that first astonishment, we learn to behold the contradictions without fleeing mentally into the refuge of a clear, all-embracing ratiocination. We learn not to let the oddities on the Tree of Life send us scrambling in terror up the Tree of Porphyry.

Now it is only here, at the end of Chapter 2, that we find the first major reference to Christianity. But note the context. Contrasting it with the spirit of the East, Chesterton asserts:

> Buddhism is centripetal, but Christianity is centrifugal: it breaks out. For the circle is perfect and infinite in its nature; but it is fixed for ever in its size; it can never be larger or smaller. But the cross, though it has at its heart a collision and a contradiction, can extend its four arms for

17. Ibid., 50–51.
18. Ibid., 49.
19. TA, 176–77.

ever without altering its shape. Because it has a paradox in its center it can grow without changing.

I'm not sure this comparison of Chesterton's really works. Why cannot a circle be larger or smaller, just like a cross? The point he is trying to make, I presume, is that the intersection involved in a cross bespeaks contrast and openness, never presuming to enclose; a circle, however, is an enclosure by its very nature. In this passage we see that it is the Christian philosophical attitude that is crucial (in more than one sense!). The Cross here is the central symbol as a sign of opposition and contradiction in the very nature of things and their interrelationships. As such, it stands opposed to the Eastern circle, the *mandala*, the *yin yang*, the *ouroboros* and the Wheel of Births. The Crucified Christ is a free development in the Christian story which grows forth in four directions from that basic mystery of the Cross.

One can go so far as to say that even if, in the Christian universe, man had not sinned and Redemption were not necessary, there would still be this tension, this holy fruitful opposition between God and His creation (vertically, so to speak), and the interpersonal communion between the Persons of the Trinity and between created persons (horizontally). The Cross is simply the Western sign of this sundering ontological distinction between God and creation, between person and person. It became the bloody Cross of Golgotha only because of creaturely disobedience. Then to the two ontological oppositions just mentioned, a third, moral opposition was added: that between heaven and hell.

We will have occasion later to see how it is precisely this first encounter with the whole world in all its imprecision, indistinction and lack of immediate logical definition, that adumbrates the notion of being in its full analogical richness. St. Thomas and his school will develop the doctrine of analogy as the great speculative underpinning of the common-sense sayings that reach out in so many ways at the articulation of a metaphysics of creation. The first idea of being, when measured against genera and species and all the logical entities designed to narrow down a meaning, is the most imprecise concept there is; but in the light of its intelligibility, every other concept and judgment shines and urgently invites the labors of reason. The fullness of being is much like the sun.

> The one created thing which we cannot look at is the one thing in the light of which we look at everything. Like the sun at noonday, mysticism explains everything else by the blaze of its own victorious invisibility.... That transcendentalism by which all men live has primarily much the position of the sun in the sky. We are conscious of it as of a kind of splendid confusion; it is something both shining and shapeless, at once a blaze and a blur.

Now the blur of a blaze may subtract from its clarity and delineation, but it can hardly be said to make it less luminous or striking. The maniac's affliction is like that of an astronomer looking at the sun through a sun-filter, permitting him to scrutinize sun-spots, while all the time ignoring "the impossible universe which stares us in the face."[20]

3. THE SUICIDE OF THOUGHT

The other sort of mental affliction destructive of the principles of thought is skepticism. Unlike the maniac, whose reason refuses to be rooted in the first sense-encounter with the universe, the skeptic suffers from a misplaced humility. Shifted away from the "organ of ambition" (where it belongs), his humility has settled upon the "organ of conviction," and suddenly his confrontation with daylight evi-

20. H, 305.

dences is blighted with misgivings. The maniac reasons too soon; the skeptic may wonder if he can reason at all.

There is a subtle affinity between these two aberrations. Both the maniac and the skeptic take mental offense at the first salute of the universe. The maniac views it askance as a beginner's playground, left for those not yet trained in the grown-up work of logic, inference, and calculation. It is too dull and formless to measure up to the canons of his intellectual sophistication. The skeptic, on the other hand, lingers in bewildered petrifaction over that same salute. It is so imprecise and mysterious that when he does finally venture a thought, only too often, it is "the thought that stops all thought" referred to in our Introduction. In other words, both err in attempting to apply reason to the pre-rational work of accepting first principles.

The maniac's specific error lies in deluding himself into reasoning out proper foundations for his own universe, which turn out finally to be a fiction. The skeptic interprets reason's failure to deduce first principles as an utter discomfiture of the endowment itself, blackening the prospects for any kind of absolute certitude. In a fit of misplaced modesty, he shrugs his shoulders and joins in Montaigne's refrain, "*Que sais-je?*" (what can I possibly know?). He cannot gauge or ascertain the authority of thought. Along with the maniac —although for different reasons—he is flustered at the world's demand to be trusted. The obvious lesson Chesterton draws from all this simply does not dawn upon the skeptic's brain, namely, that "reason is itself a matter of faith. It is an act of faith to assert that our thoughts have any relation to reality at all."

> Man, by a blind instinct, knew that if once things were wildly questioned, reason could be questioned first. The authority of priests to absolve, the authority of popes to define, the authority even of inquisitors to terrify: these

> were all only dark defences erected round one central authority, more undemonstrable, more supernatural than all—the authority of a man to think.... In so far as religion is gone, reason is going. For they are both of the same primary and authoritative kind. They are both methods of proof which cannot themselves be proved.

Here again, the reference to religion and Christianity may seem to support the claim that *Orthodoxy* is nothing but Christian apologetics. But, as before, note the platform of this apology. Christianity is cited as being a custodian of reason's proper work. As Chesterton remarks, "pull off the miter of pontifical man and lo, the head comes off with it!"

The non-rational assent required of both religion and reason is by no means an *irrational* assent. The irrational presupposes ratiocination already underway and then knowingly contradicted, either through blatant logical disobedience (like saying: "There is no such thing as truth," a statement that self-destructs in the two seconds it takes to say it), or falling short of reason through dullness of mind or intensity of emotion (such as saying: "The universe is obviously infinite," when it is not, or "Life is not worth living!", when you obviously think that it is, since you are still alive). To say reason cannot begin with reason is no more irrational than to say that lines cannot begin with lines, or dives with dives. The point is to the line, and the diving-board is to the dive, what the principle is to reason. Being a movement of thought (analogically speaking), reason presupposes, like all movement, something unmoved whence it begins its motion. Such a beginning is precisely what we call a principle. The confusions of the maniac and the skeptic are about *principles*, and the whole of *Orthodoxy* is basically a defense of them.

Now the objection that *Orthodoxy* is not written in systematic philosophical form breaks down in the face of this whole problem of principles. Trying to systematically and rationally arrive at a first principle is precisely the topsy-turvy ruse Chesterton is rebuking. Although one can reflect on one's principles and present them in an orderly and methodical way, it is in no way a demonstration of them to do this, except in the primitive, etymological sense of "showing" them to be there.

They can only be defended indirectly, and in one of three ways: 1) the arguments of those who deny first principles can indeed be rationally refuted; 2) the inner coherence of the principles can be displayed through illustration; and 3) the psychology of their genesis can be scrutinized and described. But proven they cannot be, without thereby dethroning them from their dominion by appealing to a higher scepter of evidence than theirs. Now it is in the first sort of defense in which Chesterton excels. Its major technical instrument is the so-called *reductio ad absurdum*. It belongs to that great repertoire of variations on Dr. Johnson's celebrated kick.

Chesterton performs such reductions in this chapter on four modern philosophies: materialism, idealism, evolutionism and pragmatism. His casual listing happens to follow the chronology of the appearance of the foremost exponents of each of the four schools of thought: Lamettrie, Hegel, Spencer, and James. He regards these four as comprising a "bald summary of the thought-destroying forces of our time." In each of the systems, the very utterance of the new first principle is seen to undo itself. Chesterton's reductions here are off-hand and brief. But not to pass over them entirely, let us even more briefly paraphrase them:

1) On materialism: If everything is material, so is my thought; in fact, so is this thought; that is to say, it is not really a thought at all. How then can I claim it is true?

2) On idealism: If there is no world already there before I

think about it, I, in my thinking, am not thinking *about* anything.

3) On evolutionism: If change is the absolute, then "there is no such thing as a thing"; again, nothing to think about. And besides, why should the truth of this thought not change?

The fourth one admits of no paraphrase:

4) "Pragmatism is a matter of human needs; and one of the first of human needs is to be something more than a pragmatist."

The title of this chapter is "The Suicide of Thought" because the modern philosopher is, on Chesterton's analysis, inevitably caught up in one of these intellectual self-immolations—reason pointing a pistol at itself.

To be sure, some caught on to these rationalistic booby-traps, and foreswore both the pretentious imperialism of reason in the maniac and the feeble stalemate of the skeptic. "The ultimate authority, they say, is in will, not in reason." Chesterton first casts a bemused glance at one stage of Nietzsche's thought, and makes short shrift of his proclamation of "the philosophy of the ego" by showing up a contradiction so immediate and evident, we are likely to let it pass: "To preach egoism is to practice altruism."

Turning to the more nuanced varieties of "worship of will," an absurdity is isolated which will return again and again in our author's books. It is that "idolatry of the intermediate, to the oblivion of the ultimate."[21] He grammatically characterizes this as the error of turning transitive verbs into intransitives, and, we might add, the error of taking subjects away from verbs that hang in the air without them. It is

21. TH, 13.

ubiquitous today. A typical and comical instance is found in a popular publisher's "New Age Books," advertised on the back cover as contributing to a search for "meaning, growth and change." A whole host of qualifiers, such as "which?", "what?", "of what?", "to what?", "why?", seem to vanish before the seizure of mental reverence produced at the incantation of these three semantic zeros. But we are used to it. When the word "will" is hung up in the air all by itself, we get much the same effect:

> This pure praise of volition ends in the same break up and blank as the mere pursuit of logic. Exactly as complete free thought involves the doubting of thought itself, so the acceptation of mere "willing" really paralyzes the will.... The worship of will is the negation of will. To admire mere choice is to refuse to choose.... You cannot admire will in general, because the essence of will is that it is particular.

The trouble with the exaltation of will is the same as the exaltation of reason or the exaltation of doubt—it tries to make transcendent what is intrinsically dependent and limited. The typical will-enthusiast, like Arthur Schopenhauer, wants the will to explain everything, when as a matter of fact, it can only account for anything at all by excluding everything else.

> Every act of will is an act of self-limitation. To desire action is to desire limitation. In that sense every act is an act of self-sacrifice. When you choose anything, you reject everything else. That objection, which men of this school used to make to the act of marriage, is really an objection to every act. Every act is an irrevocable selection and exclusion.

That our author now moves once again from the speculative to the moral order underscores their cohesion in his mind. These various species of limitlessness in human thought end up, in spite of their vaunted audacity and liberality, in making it a rather tame and bland business to be a human. Maniac and skeptic alike, the unrooted mind looks out at an unrooted world. One of the consequences of this is that if there are no absolutes, there can be nothing really to fight about. Mental suicide breeds political pacifism. We look on indifferently at the "fierce things fading for want of any principle to be fierce about."

At this issue of Chesterton's "rough view of recent thought," we are oncc again shown why he spotted a certain affinity of these modern philosophical quandaries with popular presentations of the perennial doctrines of the East:

> The wild worship of lawlessness and the materialistic worship of law end in the same void. Nietzsche scales staggering mountains, but he turns up ultimately in Tibet. He sits down beside Tolstoy in the land of nothing and Nirvana. They are both helpless—one because he must not grasp anything, and the other because he must not let go of anything.

4. THE ETHICS OF ELFLAND

This chapter already has a distinguished history. Besides being one of the "wittiest" of the book, the wit here is such a perfect fusion of the older and more recent meaning of the word, one is often jolted with a metaphysical vision right in the midst of a belly-laugh. But among those who have been shaken by both varieties of convulsion have been, *mirabile dictu*, members of the scientific community. As Stanley Jaki points out, one is surprised to find a large part of this chapter reprinted in 1957 in a respected anthology of *Great Essays in Science.*

> There was Chesterton in the company of Albert Einstein, Charles Darwin, Henri Fabre, J.R. Oppenheimer, Arthur Stanley Eddington, Alfred North Whitehead, and Bertrand

Russell, so many giants in mathematics, physics, and natural history. Chesterton was also in the company of such prominent interpreters of science as John Dewey, Ernest Nagel, and even T.H. and Julian Huxley.[22]

The same selection was republished in 1984.[23] Chesterton's contribution surely was not included just because it is funny.

The chapter begins with our author expressing his bewilderment over the modern business-like idea of maturation as a progressive phasing out of theory under the pressure of the demanding encroachments of practice. Chesterton's experience bespoke just the opposite. The book *Heretics* offers lucid pages on the eminent practicality of a good, abstract, and generalized theory.[24] "The most practical and important thing about a man is still his view of the universe."[25] In *Orthodoxy*, only one example is given as germane to the issues of the book. It is Chesterton's own theory, developed at great length elsewhere,[26] of democracy: (1) "that the things common to all men are more important than the things peculiar to any man. Ordinary things are more valuable than extraordinary things; nay, they are more extraordinary"; and (2) "the political instinct or desire is one of those things which they have in common." He sums it up by asserting that "the most terribly important things must be left to ordinary men themselves—the mating of the sexes, the rearing of the young, the laws of the state."

One may wonder how this fits into the argument of

22. Stanley Jaki, *Chesterton, Seer of Science* (Chicago: University of Illinois Press, 1986), 14.

23. Martin Gardner, ed., *The Sacred Beetle and Other Great Essays in Science* (Buffalo, NY: Prometheus Books, 1984), Chesterton essay, 95–104; orig. ed.: *Great Essays in Science* (New York: Pocket Books, 1957), 78–83.

24. H, 11ff.

25. Ibid., 15.

26. Joseph Sprug, *An Index to G.K. Chesterton* (Washington, DC: Catholic University Press, 1966), 98–100.

Orthodoxy. But the insight will presently be put to work. The next development of thought produces one of Chesterton's more famous passages. Turning the usual opposition of democracy to tradition inside out, he makes use of liberal principles to urge a conservative cause. Donning a Phrygian cap, Chesterton pleads that the voice of our ancestors belongs in the halls of our intellectual parliament, in defense, *à bon libéral*, of the tramped-upon rights of that unjustly suppressed majority: the dead. This fourth paragraph of Chapter 4 resists summarization; the display of insights unpacked one by one out of a logically pursued theory of democracy slowly bends the back of the reluctant liberal—by force of his own principles—into an embarrassing intellectual homage to tradition.

Now it is here that our author's strategy becomes apparent. Sharing basic tenets with the liberals of turn-of-the-century Britain (to be significantly distinguished, incidentally, from liberals of late 20th-century Britain or elsewhere!), Chesterton shows up the inconsistency in their customary ridicule of popular tradition and their rejection of anything not yet verified by the new elite of scientists. The oracles of popular tradition thus rehabilitated, we can now consult them, for these shall be our teachers in "The Ethics of Elfland."

This chapter begins Chesterton's positive presentation of "the three or four fundamental ideas which I have found for myself," which he then synthesizes as summing up his "personal philosophy or natural religion." Afterwards comes the "startling discovery that the whole thing had been discovered before." Again, it is only as a subsequent and surprising confirmation that Christianity enters the picture.

Standing on his newly won "liberal" platform of popular tradition, Chesterton proclaims that his first and most infallible lessons in thought came from fairy tales: "a certain way of looking at life, which was created in me by the fairy tales, but has since been meekly ratified by the mere facts." This "sunny country of common sense" yields two fundamental lessons in intellectual and moral sanity, and it is from such tales that all normal people derive them. Here are at last the speculative and moral principles referred to at the beginning of our study. Our author now approaches "what *ethic and philosophy* come from being fed on fairy tales." [emphasis added]

The previous chapter of *Orthodoxy* made two principal points; 1) that reason cannot be founded on reason; and 2) that will cannot be founded on will. Both of these faculties are activated by objects first greeted by something deeper and more mysterious in the soul. That deeper something is awakened long before the juncture in life when serious reflection and moral responsibility assume their ponderous roles in our experience (the "age of reason," if you will). The last chapter identified that "blaze and blur" of our first consciousness of being, but only grazed the more forbidding issue of the will's first vis-à-vis. Though far from being a voluntarist, and though intending to highlight both species of first principles in this chapter, Chesterton deliberately entitles it "The *Ethics* of Elfland." This choice of title is the result of his recognition of a much larger choice behind all choices, and finally behind the blaze of being itself.

Fairyland is a perfectly logical place, Chesterton insists. "For instance, if the Ugly Sisters are older than Cinderella, it is (in an iron and awful sense) necessary that Cinderella is younger than the Ugly Sisters. There is no getting out of it. . . . If Jack is the son of a miller, a miller is the father of Jack. Cold reason decrees it from her awful throne: and we in fairyland submit." But now we must read closely:

> But as I put my head over the hedge of the elves and began to take notice of the natural world, I observed an extraordinary thing. I observed that learned men in spectacles were talking of the actual things that happened—dawn and

> death and so on—as if they were rational and inevitable. They talked as if the fact that trees bear fruit were just as necessary as the fact that two and one trees make three. But it is not. There is an enormous difference by the test of fairyland; which is the test of the imagination. You cannot imagine two and one not making three. But you can easily imagine trees not growing fruit; you can imagine them growing golden candlesticks or tigers hanging on by the tail.
>
> We have always in our fairy tales kept this sharp distinction between the science of mental relations, in which there really are laws, and the science of physical facts, in which there are no laws, but only weird repetitions. We believe in bodily miracles, but not in mental impossibilities.

Our author is working his way back to what the philosophers call the principle of non-contradiction, that is, the axiom that something cannot both be and not be in the same way at the same time. But the long way back to this beginning is only the recapturing of an original confidence in that evidence after having lost it. That absolute first principle, with all its logical universality and necessity, is handed over to us by a world that is not logically necessary. The odd thing, however—and precisely the thing Descartes, Kant and Husserl could not see—is that you get all that wonderful logical universality and necessity only by acknowledging that an unnecessary world shows it to you. If you refuse to accept this principle as a gift, but want first to logically establish the giver by means of the yet un-received gift, you will end up by losing both. Chapter 3 showed us that we lose the gift either by trying to rationalize it, or by distrusting a strange, but ultimately veridical world. This chapter shows us that we gain the gift by opening our astonished eyes as babies, and that we feed it by listening to Mother Goose.

"It is an act of faith to believe that our reason has any relation to reality at all," we observed with our author. The baby cannot reason, but he can believe, and he does. The wonder is sustained in the child as the mother in whose lap he once sat starts telling him stories about a cat and a fiddle, and a cow jumping over the moon, and a beanstalk growing up into the clouds. Now in all these stories, Chesterton argues, "the science of mental relations" is never really misrepresented or falsified. "If the three brothers all ride horses, there are six animals and eighteen legs involved: that is true rationalism, and fairyland is full of it." The little toddler learns to know these things among the trees of the enchanted forest just as he does among the shelves at the grocery store. But the spectacle at which he gaped as a baby and over which he continues to wonder now—wanting to hear the stories over and over again—are not the mental relations, but something much more rudimentary and overwhelming: *the things related*. They are common, ordinary things—but they are amazing, and, what is more, they are bewildering. Why?

This particular point is, I believe, one for which Chesterton deserves credit for a genuine enrichment of our philosophical heritage. Let us state it now. The rest of *Orthodoxy* develops it; all of his other books, but especially *The Everlasting Man*, *St. Thomas Aquinas* and *St. Francis of Assisi*, draw it out in broad application. The idea is, in my words: Our first thought is: "There is an is!"[27] It is the first of all thoughts, the basis of all thoughts and includes all subsequent thoughts potentially in its own light. Nothing is more familiar. But, as children—and this is the clincher—we are astonished at the fact.

Why is the baby so stunned? *Why* do children love the stories for their surprises?

> This elementary wonder, however, is not a mere fancy derived from the fairy tales; on the contrary, all the fire of the fairy tales is derived from this. Just as we all like love

27. TA, 166.

tales because there is an instinct of sex, we all like astonishing tales because they touch the nerve of the ancient instinct of astonishment.

C.S. Lewis, an author who conceded his enormous philosophical and theological indebtedness to Chesterton, commented on this quality of surprise in an essay on story:

> It is the quality of unexpectedness, not the fact that delights us. It is even better the second time.... We do not enjoy a story fully at the first reading. Not till the curiosity, the sheer narrative lust, has been given its sop and laid asleep, are we at leisure to savor the real beauties. Till then, it is like wasting great wine on a ravenous natural thirst which merely wants cold wetness. The children understand this well when they ask for the same story over and over again, and in the same words. They want to have again the 'surprise' of discovering that what seemed Little Red Riding Hood's grandmother is really the wolf. It is better when you know it is coming: free from the shock of actual surprise you can attend better to the intrinsic surprisingness of the *peripeteia* [= unexpected turn of events in a story].[28]

I have included this long quote from Lewis for two reasons. First of all, it lucidly highlights the response of wonder as the principial and enduring human reaction to the surprises we encounter, most of all the surprise of the world itself. But secondly, it provides us with a perfect instance of how the whole groundwork of that very astonishment and surprise can be compromised. Without slighting the value of Lewis's considerable contribution to story-telling, I would like to draw attention to an important distinction between Chesterton's fairyland and the fantasy literature so beloved in our own times.

28. C.S. Lewis, *On Stories and Other Essays as Literature*, ed. Walter Hooper (New York: Harcourt, Brace & Jovanovich, 1982), 16–17.

Excursus No. 4: On Peter Pantheism

I mentioned before that the most influential fantasy book in the 20th century was written by Lewis Carroll. Now Lewis Carroll was a pseudonym for the 19th-century logician and mathematician Charles Dodgson. The modern world had hoped that science would prove the cosmos to be a very logical and mathematical place, and it was to experts such as Dodgson that one looked for help. In his own day, however, the imminent crises in logic and mathematics were not yet fully manifest. One thing, nonetheless, was growing more and more evident: the world was going to be either dreadfully mechanical and dull (as in Newton's synthesis)—thus sending Kantians, Romantics and Idealists off in search of an asylum for human values in the midst of that clockwork cosmos; *or* the world was going to be an unmanageable network of strange, crisscrossing energies, with an Einstein before a blackboard whitened with arcane symbols—and all this dispatching another host of refugees in search of a more hospitable habitat. Well, in either case, one popular and obvious escape-hatch—whether from cosmic tedium or from cosmic complication—was offered by that particular rigging of the imagination known as fantasy. "It is the quality of unexpectedness, not the fact that delights us," writes C.S. Lewis.

Chesterton might have pointed out, had he read this, that you had jolly well better have your fact first, if you are to have your quality at all. Since he himself wrote a number of wacky novels easily (though inaccurately) dubbed "fantastic," praised fairy tales to the skies, defended popular legend against document-mongers, and wrote book chapters with titles like "The Ethics of Elfland," he has been frequently thrown into the class of fantasy writers. And since a foremost and otherwise philosophically kindred author is none other than C.S. Lewis, one often hears his and Chesterton's name mentioned together. In several significant domains, they belong together. Their views on imaginative story-telling, however, seem to speak different languages.

For most modern fantasy writers, fantasy is a legitimate imaginative escape from the actual world of experience to an encounter with fantastic, improbable, and often impossible persons and situations. The purpose of these encounters is to teach us, or "experience" us, in a world that seems to be "more real." A sort of hazy inadequacy appears to hang over our everyday material world, and the fantasies we pursue take us off to a more three-dimensional universe. This sort of Platonic exercise is, of course, of easy apparent Christian application. Lewis expresses this general drift of mind in the following passage:

> All my deepest, and certainly all my earliest, experiences seem to be of sheer quality. The terrible and the lovely are older and solider than terrible and lovely things. If a musical phrase could be translated into words at all it would be an adjective. A great lyric is very like a long, utterly adequate, adjective. Plato was not so silly as the Moderns think when he elevated abstract nouns—that is, adjectives disguised as nouns—into the supreme realities—the Forms.[29]

In his book *The Allegory of Love*, in distinguishing the work of the "symbolist," who attempts to represent the immaterial by reading it "through its material imitations," from that of the "allegorist," who expresses the same through personifications, Lewis insists that both should "leave the given" in order to communicate the immaterial reality: "The allegorist leaves the given . . . to talk of that which is confessedly less real, which is a fiction. The symbolist leaves the given to find that which is more real."[30]

In some of the last essays he wrote, Lewis made his understanding of fantasy as clear as could be wished:

29. *Prayer: Letters to Malcolm*, ch. XVI (Glasgow: Collins, Fontana Books, 1983), 68.

30. *The Allegory of Love* (New York: Galaxy, 1958), 45.

> [T]hose who tell the story and those (including ourselves) who receive it are not thinking about any such generality as human life. Attention is fixed on something concrete and individual; on the *more than ordinary terror* [emphasis added], splendor, wonder, pity, or absurdity of a particular case. These, not for any light they might throw hereafter on the life of man, but for their own sake, are what matters.
>
> When such stories are well done we usually get what may be called hypothetical probability—what would be probable if the initial situation occurred. . . . The raison d'être of the story is that we shall weep, or shudder, or wonder, or laugh as we follow it. . . . The demand that all literature should have realism of content cannot be maintained. Most of the great literature so far produced in the world has not.

By "realism of content" is not meant the sort of photographic realism familiar from the cinema, but, as he says above, that it is about the "generality of human life." And when the predictable accusation of "escapism" enters Lewis's mind, he welcomes the idea, merely qualifying it.

> Now there is a clear sense in which all reading whatever is an escape. It involves a temporary transference of the mind from our actual surroundings to things merely imagined or conceived. This happens when we read history or science no less than when we read fiction. *All such escape is from the same thing: immediate concrete actuality. The important question is what we escape to. . . .* [emphasis added] Escape is not necessarily joined to escapism. The authors who lead us furthest into impossible regions—Sidney, Spenser, and Morris—were men active and stirring in the real world. The Renaissance and our own Nineteenth Century, periods prolific in literary fantasy, were periods of great energy.[31]

31. *An Experiment in Criticism* (Cambridge: Cambridge University Press, 1961), 64–68.

Lewis goes on in this essay to facilitate his fantasy-interpretation of fairy tale literature by assuring us that it is not actually intended for children anyway, but is more of a particular taste that has been unwisely tossed to the nursery. We cannot deal adequately with this topic in these passing observations, but what we have cited should suffice to exhibit a difference between Lewis's view of fairy tales and fantasy and what Chesterton is trying to teach us in "The Ethics of Elfland."

My point is perhaps best brought home by Lewis Carroll's comment at the end of the first chapter of *Alice in Wonderland*, in the wake of Alice's first few experiences after following the White Rabbit down the hole:

> Alice had got so much into the way of expecting nothing but out-of-the-way things to happen, that it seemed quite dull and stupid for life to go on in the common way.

At the very beginning of Chesterton's first book of essays, *The Defendant*, he lays out the basic program of defense he will pursue till his death: *the defense of the world from which Alice escapes*. Carroll's logical and mathematical world had become a drag. So down the rabbit hole to Wonderland! In a way, the whole 20th century shall celebrate and imitate that flight, beginning with Hollywood and ending in "virtual reality."

But when Chesterton stomps onto the scene, he promptly stuffs up the rabbit hole and puts up a sign with an arrow pointing at the world as it is: "Welcome to Wonderland!" It is our own fault if it has become "quite dull and stupid for life to go on in the common way." He writes: "It is a monotonous memory which keeps us in the main from seeing things as splendid as they are."[32] Unlike the escapist fantasists, he will endeavor to "provide that longest and strangest tele-

32. DE, 5.

scope—the telescope through which we could see the star upon which we dwelt. For the mind and eyes of the average man this world is as lost as Eden and as sunken as Atlantis."[33] Carroll's problem was that "he could see the logical world upside down; he could not see any other world even right side up . . . there was no sense in his nonsense."[34]

Chesterton's fairyland, as we have already seen, does indeed answer to one of Lewis's requirements for the world we must escape to, namely, that it is an extraordinary place. Only there is one enormous difference. For Chesterton, it is *this* world that is the extraordinary place, and true fairy tales, far from removing us from the real world, help us instead to see the "immediate concrete actuality" as itself the native homeland of wonder. A selection of texts from Chesterton's other works should drive the point home, without which "The Ethics of Elfland" is liable to read too much like "Through the Looking-Glass." Given in chronological order, beginning with his first book of essays in 1901, these excerpts reveal a mind quite averse to other-worldly fantasizing.

> By the cheap revolutionary it is commonly supposed that imagination is a merely rebellious thing, that it has its chief function in devising new and fantastic republics. But imagination has its highest use in a retrospective realization. . . . The prime function of imagination is to see our whole orderly system of life as a pile of stratified revolutions. In spite of all revolutionaries it must be said that the function of imagination is not to make strange things settled, so much as to make settled things strange; *not so much to make wonders facts, as to make facts wonders.*[35]
>
> . . . although people talk of the restraints of fact and the freedom of fiction, the case for most artistic purposes is quite the other way. Nature is as free as air: art is forced to

33. Ibid., 13.
34. HA, 118.
35. DE, 84.

> look probable. There may be a million things that do happen, and yet only one thing that convinces us as likely to happen.[36]
>
> ... of course a touch of fiction is almost always essential to *the real conveying of fact*, because fact, as experienced, has a fragmentariness which is bewildering at first and quite blinding at second hand. Facts have at least to be sorted into compartments and the proper head and tail given to each.[37]
>
> ... the fairy tales contain the deepest truth of the earth, *the real record of men's feelings for things*.[38]
>
> Stories of the school of Peter Pan are radiant and refreshing dreams; but they are dreams. They are dreams of somebody taking refuge from real life in an inner life of the imagination; but not necessarily of somebody believing that there is a larger universal life corresponding to that imagination.[39]
>
> It is a mark of true folklore that even the tale that is evidently wild is eminently sane.[40]
>
> ... the most wild and soaring sort of imagination: the imagination that can *see what is there*.[41]
>
> It is when a fact is thus too big for history that it overflows the surrounding facts and expresses itself in fable. Nay, it is when the fact is in a sense too solid that its very solidity breaks the framework of ordinary things; and it can only be recorded through extraordinary things like fairy tales and romances of chivalry.[42] [emphasis added in all texts]

I have included this last quote precisely because it seems on the surface to confirm the fantasy authors' position. But

36. CD, 122.
37. Ibid., 196.
38. UT, 22–23.
39. HA, 21.
40. CM, 96.
41. EM, 9.
42. RR, 91.

here again, note the all-important word "fact." Something real and actual in the world around us (say, the personality of some great conqueror or king, such as Alexander the Great or Charlemagne), suffocates in our jaded "ordinariness" and stretches its burgeoning energy into the extraordinary milieu of a legend or a fable. But here there is no escape, whether through a rabbit-hole, or a looking-glass or via a tornado trip to Munschkinland. There is rather the attempt, by extraordinary tales, of profiling anew our faded awareness of very ordinary realities.

Peter Pan is the most telling figure among the literary heralds of the fantastic. His Never-Never Land is the quintessence of the escapist delusion—not fairyland but Disneyland.

> I have always held that Peter Pan was wrong. He was a charming boy, and sincere in his adventurousness; but though he was brave like a boy, he was also a coward—like a boy. He admitted that it would be a great adventure to die; but it did not seem to occur to him that it would be a great adventure to live. If he had consented to march with the fraternity of his fellow-creatures, he would have found that there were solid experiences and important revelations even in growing up. . . .
>
> Now the mistake of Peter Pan is the mistake of the new theory of life. I might call it Peter Pantheism. It is the notion that there is no advantage in striking root. . . .[43]

We can imagine a different world, a bigger or smaller world; or a cubic world. We can imagine, and have imagined, bizarre creatures with human bodies and horses' heads, or with fifteen arms, and so on and so forth through the whole zoo of pagan mythology. Despite old Newton, we can still quite capably imagine apples falling up rather than down.

43. UD, 146.

Only the fact that the world does not exist in any one of the imaginable ways we can dream up, but is as it really is, inspires genuine wonder, for we are unable to pin down a precise reason why the Will that chose to make it thus, did not make it differently. What *did* its Maker have in mind in making it as specific as it is? This remains to us a mystery, and the old fairy tales left it at that.

The new fantasy tales, however, only too often try to manufacture their own mysteries. Closing their books can be like turning off the television set; after a vacation in fantasy-land, the return to reality is greeted with a sigh. Real life is a letdown. When you close your book of Grimms' fairy tales, on the other hand, the world you had left behind when first opening the book is now vibrating with new possibilities, and they may even keep you awake. The old tales teach us about real forests, real witches and real rivers. Here our imaginations are tempered in the fire of reality by confronting them with plenitudes of existence, which, without the oculars of poetry, might remain invisible to the jaded eye of sinners. Even the strange creatures of the fairy tales are pointing their fingers at something or someone right out there in our all-too-familiar world. "It is one thing to describe an interview with a gorgon or a griffin, a creature who does not exist. It is another thing to discover that the rhinoceros does exist and then take pleasure in the fact that he looks as if he didn't."

⊕

I mentioned before the baby and the boy, as they correspond to the beginnings of the first two stages in the order of education. With minor variations, the Western tradition has largely followed the order given by Plato in the *Republic*,[44]

44. Cf. Plato, *Republic*, bk. VII; expanded upon in Mark van Doren, *Liberal Education* (Boston, MA: Beacon Press, 1957).

which in any case is the natural order. Beginning with what Plato calls "gymnastic" education (which we might translate as the education of the "naked" sensory reality of the body), the child's first experiences of the world and of himself are trained and disciplined through physical education; secondly, the memory and the imagination are formed through the various kinds of "music" (the domain of arts governed by the Muses, including all forms of poetry, drama, music in the stricter sense, history, dance, etc.); thirdly, and only after years of gymnastic and music, the boy, now a young adolescent, may begin the formal training of the intellect with the seven liberal arts, roughly corresponding to today's verbal arts and mathematics. Of course, all three continue, in adapted proportions, throughout one's life.

The baby is totally absorbed in sensory intake. But after a certain amount of it, the child is already in need of music. The wonder has begun to wear off and poetry is needed to keep the soul attuned to reality.

> [W]hen we are very young children we do not need fairy tales: we only need tales. Mere life is interesting enough. A child of seven is excited by being told that Tommy opened a door and saw a dragon. But a child of three is excited by being told that Tommy opened a door. Boys like romantic tales; but babies like realistic tales—because they find them romantic.

Now the sense of the sequence of these two phases of education is clear enough. The baby could not yet recite "O Western Wind," even if you repeated it 100 times into its little face. But the child, on the other hand, needs and loves to sing and dance and imaginatively participate in the world as it becomes better known. All would agree, I suppose, that it is too soon for logic and science, at least until the youngster has had a few years of song and play. What Chesterton is suggesting, however, is more. This poetic education performs another task than merely a cognitive one. It not only furnishes our memory with those images, stories, paradigms, persons, and gestures on which the rational faculty will later reflect; it not only acquaints the learning child with the particulars of the world and all the surprises and incongruities with which we must live. It also has a *remedial* function.

Jacques Maritain held a conference in 1966 in which he presented what may be taken to be the final form of his theory on the intuition of being.[45] This is not the place to enter into the controversies surrounding the question, but a mere consideration of the issue he is addressing will shed considerable light on Chesterton's reflections on poetic knowledge. Our question is why he thinks we need these fairy tales to "say that apples were golden, only to refresh the forgotten moment when we found that they were green," and to "make rivers run with wine only to make us remember, for one wild moment, that they run with water." What is it that even the child has forgotten, that the baby still knew?

In brief, Maritain suggests—he modestly insists on the hypothetical status of his reflections—that the immense confusion in human thought and particularly philosophy cannot be assessed by a serious Christian philosopher without taking account of the revealed truth of original sin.

We recall in passing that Chesterton had wanted to begin with this fact in Chapter 2, regarding it to be "the only part of Christian theology which can really be proved." He means here, of course, only that the fact of serious moral disorder is an evident one, whereas the Trinity and the Incarnation are not. Maritain draws upon the traditional teaching of the four "wounds" of original sin. He singles out, in addition to the commonly highlighted disorder in the concupiscible appetite as distracting coherent human thought, also the

45. Jacques Maritain, "Réflexions sur la nature blessée et sur l'intuition de l'être," *Revue Thomiste*, LXVIII, 1968, 5–14.

hebetudo mentis, the dullness of mind resulting from sin. This involves more, Maritain holds, than mere sluggishness of the intellectual operation. The God-willed subordination of the lower to the higher faculties has resulted not only in a certain dulling of their native vitality, but also in a tendency of one faculty's proper acts to infringe on the ordered work of a cooperating faculty.

Maritain considers in particular the work of the imagination to be fraught with a certain material shock that in a way frustrates the illuminating abstractive work of the intellect. The imagination's ordered contribution to representing reality in the service of the intellect is thus easily thwarted. It gets clogged with its own products, as it were, which would bring confusion enough. But over and above this handicap, the over-excited imagination would also thwart the "intuition of being" which, in Maritain's view, the intellect in the state of innocence would naturally enjoy. Thus the mind of man would be equipped with a natural metaphysical gift, and—we may venture the extrapolation which Maritain does not make—a native sense of wonder would perdure from babyhood right through maturity and old age. Life would in effect be a fairy tale.

The issues addressed merit more attention than we can give them here. Let it suffice for our present purposes that a foremost philosopher of the 20th century has given long and careful theological thought to why the baby's wonder might indeed require a sort of reboot through the ministries of childhood's fairyland oddities.

Chesterton now articulates the first principles we have so often alluded to. Put in one of his many formulas: "The world was a shock, but it was not merely shocking; existence was a surprise, but it was a pleasant surprise." That big-eyed amazement at the world which the baby has and the child maintains with his fairy tales, the boy and the man again easily lose. For Chesterton himself, regaining it was a genuine toil in the modern, industrialized England he grew up in. But once recaptured on the adolescent pilgrimage we outlined in Part I, it set off an emotion in his soul that was to be his dominant spiritual theme:

> [T]he strongest emotion was that life was as precious as it was puzzling. It was an ecstasy because it was an adventure; it was an adventure because it was an opportunity. The goodness of the fairy tale was not affected by the fact that there might be more dragons than princesses; it was good to be in a fairy tale. The test of all happiness is gratitude; and I felt grateful, though I hardly knew to whom.

Why we should be astonished at the world at all, and why feel grateful for it at all, are two ways of asking again the disarrayed mind's query regarding its two natural bearings. Now let us turn to his special concern in this chapter with the second bearing.

The fairy tale teaches us more than that the world is strange and wonderful. It is not enough to know that we must faithfully accept the unobservable, shining blur of the sun over our heads in order to see all the clear-cut creatures about our feet. It is not enough to have learnt that the mind must first nod its humble affirmation in the awful but evident face of being, before having leave to count golden apples (or green ones) and reason out a strategy to kill a giant (or catch a rat). The universe was there first and we cannot, we may not, postpone our lives till we have figured that out. Other things we may, to a certain extent, scrutinize and know with precision and exactitude. But all this is based on reason's modest acknowledgment of its prior situation in a world of wonder. This was the first lesson of fairyland. The second is curiously similar:

> For the pleasure of pedantry I will call it the Doctrine of Conditional Joy. Touchstone talked of much virtue in an "if"; according to the elfin ethics all virtue is in an "if." The

> note of the fairy utterance always is, "You may live in a palace of gold and sapphire, *if* you do not say the word 'cow,'" or "You may live happily with the King's daughter, *if* you do not show her an onion." The vision always hangs upon a veto. All the dizzy and colossal things conceded depend upon one small thing withheld. All the wild and whirling things that are let loose depend upon the one thing that is forbidden.

This second principle, like the first, opens its light only upon the mind "of the yokel type like myself: people who gape and grin and do as they are told." Now all of us are like that as babies, and for a while, at least, as children. As should be clear by now, the "blaze and blur" of the first intellectual grasp of being as truth is simply a brilliant Chestertonian presentation of the indemonstrability of the first speculative principle. In turn, the "incomprehensible condition" of the will's first contact with being as good is a like presentation of the indemonstrability of the first moral principle, for

> the true citizen of fairyland is obeying something he does not understand at all. In the fairy tale an incomprehensible happiness rests upon an incomprehensible condition. A box is opened and all evils fly out. A word is forgotten, and cities perish. A lamp is lit, and love flies away. A flower is plucked, and human lives are forfeited. An apple is eaten, and the hope of God is gone.

The classic scholastic formula for the first moral principle compresses the whole paradox, here so strikingly dramatized by Chesterton, into the compact imperative of a single gerundive; *bonum est facie***ndum** (the good is that which ought to be done). The good is, like the truth of being, a first. No one can finally account for this "oughtness," this "-**ndum**." "The idea of choice is an absolute and no one can really get behind it."[46] It is so fundamental that someone as

46. AS, 104.

gifted as Immanuel Kant could attempt to root all certitude in such a moral imperative, as we saw in the last part of our book. He is at least right that it is something irreducibly basic. Getting beneath it would mean that it was not a first, just as getting to a floor beneath the cellar would mean that it was not the cellar after all.

For Chesterton, however, the wonder of this first moral principle is not just that it is fundamental, but that it is such a vulnerable foundation. Although it is evident that the good must be done, we do not have to do it. The teasing paradox is captured by remarking that that which *ought* to be done does not *have* to be done. This is the peculiar fascination of happiness. The fairy tales teach that its attainment is only achieved through the seemingly arbitrary doorway of petty taboos or puzzling commands: Beauty's father must not pick a rose; Cinderella must be back by midnight. Children pick this up with uncanny matter-of-factness: "Step on a crack and break your mother's back!" In the fairy tales, the very fragility of this all-important condition is often expressed in the image of glass:

> [T]his thin glitter of glass everywhere is the expression of the fact that the happiness is bright but brittle, like the substance most easily smashed by a housemaid or a cat. And this fairy-tale sentiment also sank into me and became my sentiment towards the whole world. I felt and feel that life itself is as bright as the diamond, but as brittle as the window-pane; and when the heavens were compared to the terrible crystal I can remember a shudder. I was afraid that God would drop the cosmos with a crash.

Precisely this precarious pivot of every moral decision seems to put moral security beyond mortal reach. But Chesterton pursues the metaphor of glass one step further:

> Remember, however, that to be breakable is not the same as to be perishable. Strike a glass, and it will not endure an

instant; simply do not strike, and it will endure a thousand years. Such, it seems, was the joy of man, either in Elfland or on earth; the happiness depended on not doing something which you could at any moment do and which, very often, it was not obvious why you should not do.

Having reached this unsettling discovery, like suddenly realizing that you are gamboling along on a one-inch layer of ice, Chesterton responds surprisingly:

> [To] me this did not seem unjust. If the miller's third son said to the fairy, "Explain why I must not stand on my head in the fairy palace," the other might fairly reply, "Why, if it comes to that, explain the fairy palace." If Cinderella says, "How is it that I must leave the ball at twelve?," her godmother might answer, "How is it that you are going there till twelve?". . . . It seemed to me that existence was itself so very eccentric a legacy that I could not complain of not understanding the limitation of the vision when I did not understand the vision they limited. The frame was no stranger than the picture.

Chesterton's "fairy-godmother philosophy" grounds itself in a fundamental attitude of humility. To see the truth and to want the good, you must first accept them—like a gift. Only then can you have them—like a possession. Here already we must insist, as Chesterton's reaction above testifies, that this acceptance is far from being a mere shot in the dark. Being and first principles are evident to the mind; there is no darkness about them at all. It is just that we are quite able (even in sophisticated philosophical form) to confuse ourselves to such a degree that we become convinced that they are not evident (all the time using them in the attempt to discredit them).

But, unmolested by such contrived confusion, their apprehension is not an act of faith; it is an act of high-noon intellectual vision. The "faith" and "belief" Chesterton spoke of is only regarding the skeptic's curious and prying question: "How do you know that your mind's report of evidence can be trusted to begin with?" Again, we cannot get behind this, so we must answer: the report can be trusted because the evidence, though *in* the mind, is not really *of* it. The trouble with the maniac and the skeptic is not really that they are out of their minds, but rather that they are far too much in their minds, and busy breeding thoughts of their own making. When an occasional brush with reality pulls them off this merry-go-round, they are dizzy and disoriented and certain of nothing. But in our saner moments, we know the world to be true because, in my own formulation:

> *the world has come into our mind and we, in turn, have gone out into the world and found the two to agree. On the witness of the two the evidence stands.*

If this does not satisfy the skeptic, he can join Descartes, Kant, and Husserl in their endless search of proof for principles, like men insisting on having a thing photographed before daring to look at it. Chesterton stands rather with Aristotle, who insists that "each of the first principles should command belief in and by itself."[47]

This other first principle, dealing with the matter of will, is necessarily less luminous to the mind's touch, but hardly less convincing. By taking these two points of departure apart for skeptical analysis, one kills to dissect. And we lose our secure hold on them out of a false need for rational "scientific, up-to-date" guarantees for truths perfectly capable of standing on their own. Indeed, as pointed out before, the very attempt at such rational justification seems to undermine that original conviction, like someone asking you to prove that you are standing before them. You can't give reasons to someone afflicted with that kind of doubt; all you

47. Aristotle, *Topics*, I, 1, 100b 21; trans. W.A. Prichard-Cambridge, in R. McKeon, *The Basic Works of Aristotle* (New York: Random House, 1971), 188.

can do is jump up and down, shake them by the shoulders, glare into their face, and await the epiphany.

Twentieth-century man, with his overweening pride in scientific solutions to everything, required humility not to begrudge the unaided senses of the most uneducated person the high privilege of establishing the bedrock of all evidence. For that is what one does by quietly ascertaining the existence of the universe. Self-effacement must needs precede the vision of the world. As Chesterton wrote in his first book, *The Defendant*:

> Humility is the luxurious art of reducing ourselves to a point, not to a small thing or a large one, but to a thing with no size at all, so that to it all the cosmic things are what they really are—of immeasurable stature.[48]

And afterwards in *Heretics*, he continues the thought:

> The man who destroys himself creates the universe. To the humble man, and to the humble man alone, the sun is really a sun; to the humble man, and to the humble man alone, the sea is really a sea.[49]

In summary, this humble bow to the first salute of the universe unfolds in our minds the "two most essential doctrines," that, first:

> this world is a wild and startling place, which might have been quite different, but which is quite delightful; second, that before this wildness and delight one may well be modest and submit to the queerest limitations of so queer a kindness.

The modern world turned out, of course, to oppose Chesterton on both scores. "Men in spectacles" were claiming that the world in all its gift-like specificity *had* to be as it is, and

48. DE, 136.
49. H, 165.

we, in turn, *have* to act as we act. Here is where our author exercised the first sort of defense of the first principles by refuting the refutations. All the recurrences cited as evidence for this necessity were only, as Hume had shown long ago, rosters of empirical impressions making no more than a credible promise of future continuation. Intrinsic necessity, on the other hand, speaks a different language altogether.

Chesterton saw that there was no absolute necessity in the daily sunrise, nor in the endless iteration of the form of grass blades, nor in the fall of all the apples in the world. Scientists have since granted, as anyone can read today in popular science, that the so-called "laws of nature" are but "a stated regularity in the relations or order of phenomena in the world . . . [and that] a law of nature has no logical necessity; rather it rests directly or indirectly upon the evidence of experience."[50] But what about all the regularity and order, and all those repetitions? If they are not necessary laws, what are they? Here Chesterton helps us more than Hume:

> I speak here only of an emotion, and of an emotion at once stubborn and subtle. But the repetition in nature seemed sometimes to be an excited repetition, like that of an angry schoolmaster saying the same thing over and over again. The grass seemed signaling to me with all its fingers at once; the crowded stars seemed bent upon being understood. The sun would make me see him if he rose a thousand times. The recurrences of the universe rose to the maddening rhythm of an incantation, and I began to see an idea.

We must remind ourselves that Chesterton is not claiming to give a logical demonstration of principles. Instead, his desultory discoveries in the course of a variety of experiences slowly orchestrate into one resounding conviction. He

50. As had become a commonplace by the 1974 edition of the *Encyclopaedia Britannica*, 15th ed., Micropaedia VI, 89.

somewhere compares this to someone studying up-close the details of a large painting and suddenly putting them all together in his mind with the shock of recognizing a huge face staring back at him.

> I had always vaguely felt facts to be miracles in the sense that they are wonderful: now I began to think them miracles in the stricter sense that they were *willful.* I mean that they were, or might be, repeated exercises of some will. . . . And this pointed to a profound emotion always present and subconscious; that this world of ours has some purpose; and if there is a purpose, there is a person. I had always felt life as a story: and if there is a story there is a story-teller.

But this sense that there was someone, or even many someones, behind the universe—a truth echoed in all the popular myths of the world—was likewise slighted by the modern mind. Over against the notion of such little, limiting wills and the concomitant focus and plans and particular meanings involved, the modern scientist had begun expostulating till he was blue in the face on the huge, overwhelming, gigantesque and utterly awe-inspiring vastness of the universe. Ironically, behind this over-stated emphasis on magnitude lies often enough a blanket denial of any and all transcendence.

Chesterton leads us instead very close to the theme of the "second navigation" of the great Plato. It is with this metaphor, in one of his dialogues,[51] that Plato portrays his philosophical discovery of the transcendent order of being. It is arguable that this was his single greatest contribution to the Western tradition which Chesterton is defending. Determining that previous thinkers had unsuccessfully accounted for the physical world on the first launch of dialectical exploration on a purely immanent basis, Plato sets out again. He

51. Plato, *Phaedo*, 99, c–d.

ascertains that there is necessarily a world beyond which does cause (in some way) the immanent world we directly experience.

Chesterton is suggesting here, however, in poetical as well as rhetorical language, that the common and normal experience of "significance" in the world already gives us a strong implicit grasp of some transcendent dimension. And if the world "means" something, there must be someone beyond it who intends that meaning. It would take hours of philosophical work to resolve this clue into finely honed arguments in full syllogistic form. Here again, the humble first encounter with the universe, when true to its first principles and happy to take them on their immediate evidence, reveals the deepest mysteries to the eyes of a child.

The stubbornly sophisticated eye, on the other hand, stops gazing and starts squinting. It simply cannot shake itself loose from the vision of that long string of zeros modern science has come up with (1,000,000,000's of light-years of distance, 1,000,000's of years of evolution, and so on). The poet's universe with its "freshness and airy outbreak" inspires instead a litany of astonished "Oh's!". It seems that the scientific universe, with its "larger and larger windowless rooms," inspires no more than a calculated readout of magnitudes, mechanically uttered in digits—the "Oh's!" of exultation being replaced by the zeros of computation.

The trouble with all the scientist's zeros, like the trouble with the maniac's reason-gone-wild, is that both the zeros and the syllogisms braid themselves together into a chain that chokes them both.

> In fairyland there had been a real law; a law that could be broken, for the definition of a law is something that can be broken. But the machinery of this cosmic prison was something that could not be broken; for we ourselves were only a part of its machinery. We were either unable to do things or we were destined to do them.

Stanley Jaki has summarized the essential point as follows:

> The specificity or queerness of things, both when taken singly and when taken together, that is, as a cosmos or universe, was in Chesterton's judgment the means *par excellence* to restore sensitivity for the real. Such sensitivity was a commitment to a reality much more than sheer logic, and this is the reason Chesterton spoke not of the logic but of the ethics of Elfland. Consideration of the specificity was also the means of making it dawn on the onlooker that a ubiquitous and all-embracing specificity is the result of a choice transcending the cosmos, a choice which is therefore the sole privilege of a Creator.[52]

And applying all this to man, Jaki continues:

> Once the ontological emptiness of the notion of scientific law was exposed and a realist grasp of existence achieved, reality could be seen as the product of a superior will and therefore a place germane to the exercise of free human will.[53]

The next chapter of *Orthodoxy* will take us further along this road. But as Chesterton gives a sort of summary at the end of the present chapter, let us attempt at this juncture to make a provisional distillation of what I hold to be the book's underlying philosophical theses:

1) "The world does not explain itself . . . the thing is magic, true or false." The scientist's expanded universe—today we would add the expand*ing* universe—does not explain, but only increases the number of cubic light-years that need explanation. The world seems to be speaking a very specific language, but we have either forgotten it or have yet to learn it. (Here the philosophical concept of *creation* is adumbrated.)

52. Jaki, 20.
53. AB, 53.

2) There is "something personal in the world, as in a work of art; whatever it means is meant violently." The language spoken by the world is obviously spoken by someone and to someone, and "I thought this purpose beautiful in its old design." (Here the philosophical concept of *person* is approached.)

3) "The proper form of thanks to it is some form of humility and restraint . . . we owe an obedience to whatever made us . . ." and, that "in some way all good was a remnant to be stored and held sacred out of some primordial ruin." (Here the philosophical concept of *freedom* and its correlate, *authority*, are intimated.)

Chesterton's two principles show their fecundity in the generation and gestation of these three basic concepts of a philosophy that found its bearing in a Christian universe. That he would never have arrived at them without living in the West is clear. Christian civilization was suffering, but it still evidenced a certain "Robinson Crusoe syndrome." The full ship of Christendom had sunk, so it seemed, but like Crusoe, modern man has found a limited but interesting assortment of flotsam. Among the residual cargo are the notions of free will, of creation from nothing, and of personal love.

The concepts are natural, accessible to reason. But, as we shall examine in a later chapter, they have unfolded their full content only in a specifically Christian culture. Because that culture is on the decline, they need today not only exposition, but defense as well. It will take a man of the gifts of Chesterton to be able to "work them out on his own" and put them in such brilliant profile. But most of us will find ourselves welcoming them like long-lost coordinates of our inmost mental map. They are the proper domain of the Christian philosopher: not holes to be filled by Christian revelation, but the "soils for the seeds of doctrine."

5. THE FLAG OF THE WORLD

"A man belongs to this world before he begins to ask if it is nice to belong to it. He has fought for the flag, and often won heroic victories for the flag long before he has ever enlisted. To put shortly what seems the essential matter, he has a loyalty long before he has any admiration." Following the enchanted childhood encounter with the world come the doughty boyhood engagements. There is a loose chronological backdrop to this development of human knowledge from the baby to the child to the boy. Chesterton wrote of the last:

> Boyhood is a most complex and most incomprehensible thing. Even when one has been through it, one does not understand what it was. A man can never quite understand a boy, even when he has been the boy. There grows all over what was once the child a sort of prickly protection like hair; a callousness, a carelessness, a curious combination of random and quite objectless energy with a readiness to accept conventions.[54]

The boy's love for adventure stories reflects a growing response deep within the resources of a maturing mind. It is the sense of loyalty. In contrast, the erection of the intimidating alternatives of pessimism and optimism is typical muddle-headed modernity to Chesterton.

The trouble with the calculating scientist, often enough, was that he was not "fond of the universe." Your first confrontation with the quite specific make-up and detailed rules of the world should have made it clear to your dawning consciousness that this world is special, and ought to be appreciated in a special way. In brief, it is *your* cosmos. Who cares how big it is? What other cosmos are you comparing it to?

Indeed, as Chesterton urged at the end of the last chapter, any genuine fondness for the world would incline us to use

54. Ibid., 53.

diminutives. If you loved this dear little cosmos with its cute galaxies, and all those snuggling billions of light-years, you would feel the same way towards it as you do (or should) towards your family or fatherland. "The point is not that this world is too sad to love or too glad not to love; the point is that when you do love a thing, its gladness is a reason for loving it, and its sadness a reason for loving it more."

The universe, in the last analysis, is improved upon neither by the optimist nor by the pessimist. They are equally ineffective for they are equally blind. As someone has pointed out, the optimist is the man who thinks this is the best of possible worlds, and the pessimist is simply the man who agrees with him. They both are equally immobilized by their essentially identical determinisms. The cosmic patriot, however, lavishes the world with decoration, not because it is immaculate in order to award it, nor because it is ugly in order to cover it, but because it is loved in order to indulge it. But the very same love may just as readily cause him to criticize it. "The devotee is entirely free to criticize; the fanatic can safely be a skeptic. Love is not blind; that is the last thing that it is. Love is bound; and the more it is bound the less it is blind."

We have noted before the recurrent link-up in the mind of Chesterton of moral evil with mental error. I must insist that this correlation can be urged only in the matter of principles, which is of course the topic at hand. It is surely possible to be intellectually in error, at least in some matters, and still be a saint. Likewise, mental brilliance and accuracy can cohabit quite maddeningly with moral corruption. All that Chesterton is suggesting is that one's initial speculative registration of the universe demands an immediate act of moral humility, and a docility of will before a world that transcends us.

The further back we drive our speculative issues, the more principial and absolute their practical offspring become. If the denial of the first greeting of the universe issues in a failure to love it and stand to its flag, disobedience to its mysterious "condition" (the prohibition of the apple, the moral imperative, etc.) issues, if carried out to its horrible consummation, in suicide—but no longer the mere self-slaughter of thought. Just as the "thought that stops all thought" was a kind of ultimate intellectual transgression, so it is in the ontological sphere with corporal suicide:

> Not only is suicide a sin, it is the sin. It is the ultimate and absolute evil, the refusal to take an interest in existence; the refusal to take the oath of loyalty to life. The man who kills a man, kills a man. The man who kills himself, kills all men; as far as he is concerned he wipes out the world. . . . There is not a tiny creature in the cosmos at whom his death is not a sneer.

Just a few years after Chesterton's death in 1936, Albert Camus published *The Myth of Sisyphus*, in the opening pages of which we find the famous line Chesterton would no doubt have applauded:

> There is only one truly serious philosophical problem, that of suicide. To judge whether life is or is not worth the while living responds to the fundamental question of philosophy.[55]

One of Chesterton's favorite literary creations was Innocent Smith, who, among other things, held pistols up to the heads of professing pessimists, offering to put the last practical link in the chain of their dismal logic.

Now this peculiar dual fruit of cosmic patriotism: to "hate [the cosmos] enough to change it, and yet love it enough to think it worth changing," laid out one more mental landscape in Chesterton's mind over which Christian doctrine then strode with conspicuous grace. On all possible issues,

55. Albert Camus, *The Myth of Sisyphus*, trans. J. O'Brien, 1955.

Christianity played it from both sides. St. Anthony of the Desert's eremitism was hailed because he hated life enough (in this world) to give it up. Mother Teresa's life is hailed because she loved life enough to go about saving it. The believer could be both fiercely against the world and fiercely for it—all out of the selfsame love.

The Christian creed also responded harmoniously to the discovery that we must first look out into the world before we look inward into ourselves. As Chesterton would later write in *The Everlasting Man*:

> Christianity does appeal to a solid truth outside itself: to something which is in that sense external as well as eternal. It does declare that things are really there; or in other words, that things are really things. In this Christianity is at one with common sense; but all religious history shows that this common sense perishes except where there is Christianity to preserve it.[56]

At this earlier date, however, Chesterton has yet to develop these ideas fully. The truths are there, but still housed in the imaginative order. This is itself an illustration of his own thesis. *Orthodoxy* is full of Chesterton as the baby, the child and the boy. The thoughts in the above lines, penned in 1925, came out like this almost twenty years earlier, in *Orthodoxy* (1908):

> Christianity came into the world, firstly in order to assert with violence that a man had not only to look inwards, but to look outwards, to behold with astonishment and enthusiasm a divine company and a divine captain. The only fun of being a Christian was that a man was not left alone with the Inner Light, but definitely recognized an outer light, fair as the sun, clear as the moon, terrible as an army with banners.

Of course, the imaginative grasp is not just succeeded by

56. EM, 155.

the abstract, intellectual resolution, but is rather enriched by it. No one will insist so strongly on this as Thomas Aquinas, who identifies a specifically human component in cognition to be the "return to the phantasm."[57] At any rate, Chesterton's imaginative gift remains to the end, only to be sobered by a more discursive exposition in the later works.

In the present chapter, our author moves from Christianity's confirmation of his instinct of cosmic loyalty and its outward-bound mental inclinations to two ways of undoing it all. They both echo the suspicion of a personal, meaningful presence in the world. One of those ways is to seek the God within. The other is to seek the God without, that is, in Nature. Neither goes beyond. The second navigation is canceled and bogus claims are tendered that there has been landfall after all. Both these attempts are only briefly described here, the first in relation to Quakerism and Stoicism, and the second in relation to pagan nature worship. They will expand into full expositions in *The Everlasting Man*.[58] But in *Orthodoxy*, the two typical errors merely highlight man's frantic search for some satisfactory personal reciprocity in the cosmos whose flag he flies.

This particular dilemma of trying to seek the personal source of our feeling about the world either in ourselves or in nature was addressed head-on by Christianity. It was done through the doctrine of creation. The reason why the world does not explain itself is the same as the reason why the chair or the table does not explain itself. It is made. And it is clearly not an outgrowth or an evolution of its craftsman. Chairs do not grow on carpenters like noses and ears. As the artist and the artifact, so the world and its Maker are distinct.

> This answer was like the slash of a sword; it sundered; it did not in any sense sentimentally unite. Briefly, it divided

57. *Summa Theologiae*, q. 84, a.7.
58. EM, 1, chs. 4–7.

> God from the cosmos. . . . This principle that all creation and procreation is a breaking off is at least as consistent through the cosmos as the evolutionary principle that all growth is a branching out. A woman loses a child even in having a child. All creation is separation. Birth is as solemn a parting as death.

Again, the faith comes into the picture, but not as the answer to a question, or the solution to a problem. It would be more accurate to call it the baptizing of the question and the transfiguration of the problem. This is what we mean when we say that the questions of God are more satisfying than the answers of men. The tension of the need to be at once fiercely for and fiercely against the universe, to have an almost jingoistic fervor for the big spectacle and at the same time a *contemptus mundi* ("contempt" for the world), is not best borne by being resolved or leveled out. It is best borne by being shouldered foursquare. The doctrine of creation showed how "one could be both happy and indignant without degrading one's self to be either a pessimist or an optimist. On this system one could fight all the forces of existence without deserting the flag of existence. *One could be at peace with the universe and yet be at war with the world.*" [emphasis added]

The centrality of the realization of the truth of creation to Chesterton's thought can hardly be overstated. He ends this chapter by describing how, once this was seen, all remaining puzzle pieces in his mental encounter with the world dovetailed. Comparing his grasp of the world and the Christian tradition to two huge and apparently unconnected machines, once the linkup of the hole of "finding a way of loving the world without trusting it," with the spoke of the truth of creation, "all the other parts fitted and fell in with an eerie exactitude. . . . Instinct after instinct was answered by doctrine after doctrine."

Here our author will appear to finally betray intellectual

kinship with the Blondelian position. After all, the last named image for the most crucial doctrine is precisely one of holes and corresponding protrusions. But here we must look at the text with care. Chesterton wishes to relate "an experience impossible to describe." The "as if" of the image that follows is intended to convey Christianity's sudden confirmation of his common-sense philosophy, once the doctrine of creation was properly grasped. Two unwieldy metallic constructs suddenly clicking together in a totally surprising way was the image, and a good one, that came to his mind. It is, however, the confirmation and continuation of already present "instincts," as he terms them, that mark this correspondence. It is precisely a *co*rrespondence between two dimensions, and not merely the response to a question.

This is matched remarkably by the teaching of Thomas Aquinas that the truth of creation in time is attainable by the natural intellect, but *de facto*, never was attained until Biblical revelation helped guide the philosophizing mind to this arduous metaphysical conclusion.[59]

So here at the end of this chapter, with its arpeggio of ascending realizations, finding its climax in the truth of creation, we find again our three pivotal notions of true philosophy:

1. "God was personal..."
2. "...had made a world separate from Himself."
3. "I was right when I felt that the roses were red by some sort of choice: it was the divine choice."

59. Garrigou-Lagrange, *Reality* (St. Louis, MO: Herder, 1950), 124ff.

6. THE PARADOXES OF CHRISTIANITY

Chesterton's "only purpose in this chapter is to show that whenever we feel there is something odd in Christian theology, we shall generally find that there is something odd in the truth." He had begun five chapters ago with the discovery that if you are not ready to take the universe as it is—obscurities and all—you will never arrive at clarity about anything. The "blaze of being" first shining on the mind and the "crazy thread of a condition" upon which the happiness of the will hung, both were evident enough, but no less perplexing. We followed our author's further exploration of these two evidences and saw how they inspired his "fairy-godmother philosophy," which Stanley Jaki calls his "epistemological ethos."[60]

The "ethics" of Elfland simply contain the discovered duties of astonished gratitude at being placed in such a gratuitous world, and the resulting alacrity with which one submits to "the queerest limitations of so queer a kindness." In that chapter, and carried still further in the following, is the next discovery, namely, that full intellectual anchorage in these two first principles primes the mind for a triply articulated insight: The world is (1) freely (2) made (3) by someone. This had been the direction in which Chesterton's mental instincts had been moving, and the securing of the first principles made them move even faster. Christianity merely crowned them with the full trumpet blast of dogma. But what had been crowned were not placid patterns on a mosque, but busy, warring statues around a baroque altar. The concepts bred in this world seem almost to be at war with each other. Christianity simply made it clear that they were not contradictory, but something far stranger and mysterious to the mind: they were *paradoxical.*

60. Jaki, 23.

You can learn to live with contradictions on a short-term basis. They are temporary illogicalities doomed by their own self-negation. Their days are always numbered, and longevity is rare. Paradoxes, however, endure. Free of true contradiction, they have inherent vitality and positivity. But beyond that they possess a sometimes enervating elasticity and buoyancy, able to spring back all the more swiftly through the seesaw of their double affirmation. The wider world they stretch in—and without crashing into each other—is the vast universe of the analogous concept of being. That concept, however, must first be unerringly fixed in its first principles, if all the loaded opposites of a paradoxical cosmos are to be turned loose to dance, and not to collide.

In other words, once the law of non-contradiction was seen to be an intellectual absolute, and the "sign of contradiction" (the Tree of Temptation) a moral absolute, the other oppositions stopped warring and began harmonizing. The harmony, however, was no tame organum, but rather an animated and complex Bachian counterpoint. How such a restless interplay can still be harmonious will be the subject of this chapter.

> Madly as Christians might love the martyr or hate the suicide, they never felt these passions more madly than I had felt them long before I dreamed of Christianity. Then the most difficult and interesting part of the mental process opened, and I began to trace this idea through all the enormous thoughts of our theology. The idea was that which I had outlined touching the optimist and the pessimist; that we want not an amalgam or compromise, but both things at the top of their energy; love and wrath both burning.

It had not felt right—indeed it had not worked—to merely exult in the world, any more than to merely renounce it. And any blend of the two seemed insipid. We hunger for leave to do both, and Christianity surprisingly allowed us to do just that. No other religion or philosophy did. We could turn to creation's treasures and proclaim: God created them—so exult! But then we could also add: You have polluted it—so renounce! The Church had somehow married the two: she had the somber season of Lent, but she also had Easter; she made her people fast, but then she turned around and commanded them to feast.

Back in the natural order again, we find a similar reciprocation: the mind says the world is there; then the mind says the world is not *all* there. Struggling with the puzzle of contingency, the mind needs to affirm what it sees, but at the same time, and in the exigencies of the same vision, affirm what it cannot see, but wants to see. The world does not look like an Absolute, but the mind wants an Absolute it can look at. Denying the world denies the seeing, but absolutizing the world denies the Absolute. What to do? Again, the doctrine of creation gives the answer:

The world is not absolute, but it was freely created by the Absolute, and participates in a finite way in His being. Thus in looking at the world, one learns something about Him; but none of its lessons is more pressing than that you will have to look beyond the world—if that be possible—to look the Absolute in the face. The monist (he who teaches that only one sovereign substance can possibly exist) may advance the understandable objection that finite beings who are not God, nor parts of God, would seem to limit His infinity by not being embraced by His own perfections. But St. Thomas "solved" the dilemma thus: after God created the world, it is true that there was no more being than before—there was not; but there were more *beings*. Like new objects reflecting old light, the light itself remains the same—just caught, refracted and reflected in new ways. All this is worthy of tomes of exposition. But this already allows us to see that paradox lies not only in the style of the jolly journalist, but also at the heart of the Dumb Ox's metaphysics.

Chesterton's manifold use of paradox is deservedly celebrated. Its underlying speculative roots, however, are seldom appreciated. As he sees paradox, it is precisely this cohabitation of fierce opposites which experience most audibly bespeaks. And it is this which Christianity, in turn—and Christianity alone—repeats, laying bare in a series of startling doctrines its ontological roots. The most telling doctrine, as we saw in the last chapter, is creation. And the deepest secret it tells is the paradoxical make-up of reality itself. Created realities are by necessity composed of rival principles: quantity and quality, subject and act, substance and accident, matter and form, and ultimately, for all, even spiritual creatures: essence and act of being. All these result necessarily from the basic ontological "opposition" between Creator and creature. Here lie the notions that St. Thomas expands into his metaphysics of contingent being. At its basis, however, lie the paradoxes Chesterton identifies.

Our author continues in this chapter to trot out a host of contrarieties all triggered off by human cognition and volition, and then picked up in a new harmony by Christian revelation. But among these, a still subtler feature is detected:

> The real trouble with this world of ours is not that it is an unreasonable world, nor even that it is a reasonable one. The commonest kind of trouble is that it is nearly reasonable, but not quite. Life is not an illogicality; yet it is a trap for logicians. It looks just a little more mathematical and regular than it is; its exactitude is obvious, but its inexactitude is hidden; its wildness lies in wait. . . . It is this silent swerving from accuracy by an inch that is the uncanny element in everything. . . . [T]his element of the quiet and incalculable.

This distinctive cast of common experience is familiar, indeed so familiar, we scarcely advert to it. Chesterton points it out with a kind of boyish wonder, drawing its peculiar profile before our minds. He makes us wonder "*Why* is it that things are like that?" He induces us to suspect that some person is behind this teasing remissness. "It seems a sort of secret treason in the universe."

As we should by now expect, Chesterton discovers that Christianity mirrors this feature too, so much so "that its plan suits the secret irregularities and expects the unexpected." Chesterton does not pursue this correspondence here for all its worth. It is actually the last straw in his mind's register of Christian confirmations, overwhelming by its very subtlety. Being thus led to a kind of resourceless surrender, he remarks that "a man is not really convinced of a philosophic theory when he finds that something proves it. He is only really convinced when he finds that everything proves it."

He finds himself happily cornered by a concert of Christian evidences, each in tune with all the others. Now at precisely this moment, Chesterton makes an observation which drives home, as nowhere else in the book, the affinity of the supernatural suasions for Christian revelation with the natural first evidences of common sense. He is describing this in a paragraph that really is Christian apologetics, but its whole persuasive power derives from its being framed in the context of natural first principles.

> It is very hard for a man to defend anything of which he is entirely convinced. It is comparatively easy when he is only partly convinced. He is partially convinced because he found this or that proof of the thing, and he can expound it . . . the more converging reasons he finds pointing to this conviction, the more bewildered he is if asked suddenly to sum them up . . . that very multiplicity of proof which ought to make reply overwhelming makes reply impossible.

What Chesterton writes elsewhere about first principles and common sense echoes this characterization clearly enough:

> . . . the thousand converging things that make up common sense.[61]
>
> . . . the dumb certainties of experience.
>
> . . . obvious to sense, it is obscure to language. The stupidest person can feel it; the cleverest person cannot define it.[62]
>
> The thing that cannot be defined is the first thing; the primary fact. It is our arms and legs, our pots and pans, that are indefinable. The indefinable is the indisputable. The man next door is indefinable, because he is too actual to be defined. And there are some to whom spiritual things have the same fierce and practical proximity; some to whom God is too actual to be defined.[63]
>
> The word that has no definition is the word that has no substitute.[64]
>
> Precisely because the word is indefinable, the word is indispensable.[65]

It is to the exhaustive self-evidence of the world and its very first lessons that Chesterton turns to test the credentials of the Christian faith. And he finds the two persuasions match. The matter is obviously different, but the method is much the same. He feels able to start with anything and find a convincing path leading back to the Church; just as one can pick up any object and illustrate the truth of being.

To repeat, Chesterton began his quest of common sense by simply noting a fundamental acceptation that illuminates everything else. He then finds that this basis leads to the Herculean harmonization of the feistiest antagonisms on earth. He does not refer explicitly to the East in this chapter, save a single allusion to China. Nonetheless, that pale shadow-image to the colored, boldly outlined vision painted in these

61. SS, 32.
62. *Collected Works* (San Francisco: Ignatius Press, 1986), vol. XXVIL, 483.
63. CD, 1.
64. Ibid., 2.
65. Ibid.

most vibrant pages of the book, is all too present. Two chapters on he will again forcibly enjoin the East-West opposition as fundamental to the book's thesis. Here, without direct advertence, he returns again to his view of the false harmony of Eastern fusion, absorption and oceanic homogenization as opposed to Western enhancement, coronation and fruition of the God-given oppositions. A long text from another book along this same line will make this clear:

> The Eastern mysticism is an ecstasy of unity; the Christian mysticism is an ecstasy of creation, that is of separation and mutual surprise. The latter say, like St. Francis, "My brother fire and my sister water"; the former says, "Myself fire and myself water." Whether you call the Eastern attitude an extension of oneself into everything or a contraction of oneself into nothing is a matter of metaphysical definition. The effect is the same, an effect which lives and throbs throughout all the exquisite arts of the East. This effect is the thing called rhythm, a pulsation of pattern, or of ritual, or of colors, or of cosmic theory, but always suggesting the unification of the individual with the world. But there is quite another kind of sympathy—the sympathy with a thing because it is different.... The supreme instance of this divine division is sex, and that explains (what I could never understand in my youth) why Christendom called the soul the bride of God. For real love is an intense realization of the "separateness" of all our souls. The most heroic and human love-poetry of the world is never mere passion; precisely because mere passion really is a melting back into Nature, a meeting of the waters. And water is plunging and powerful; but it is only powerful downhill. The high and human love-poetry is all about division rather than identity; and in the great love-poems even the man as he embraces the woman sees her, in the same instant, afar off; a virgin and not a stranger.[66]

66. MM, 194–96.

It is this marvelous manner of getting "over the difficulty of combining furious opposites, by keeping them both, and keeping them both furious" that is the peculiar endowment of a mind tempered by the lessons of first principles. The oppositions in reality are not canceled, but enhanced. In most of them (such as God/creature, man/woman, up/down, big/small, etc.) both can and must be kept, and kept "furious," i.e., fully themselves. But there is another opposition, too, and this one raises challenging questions. I mean the opposition between good and evil.

The way in which Chesterton approaches this subject is one of the masterstrokes of his paradoxical insight. What a temptation here to a mind so set on keeping "the paradox of parallel passions" in full evidence! How easy to try to "integrate" the energies of good and those of evil in a grand and definitive *coincidentia oppositorum* (coincidence of opposites, after Nicholas Cusano)! Could Chesterton not chime in with Mr. Capra in his approving exposition of Taoism?

> [W]henever you want to retain anything, you should admit in it something of its opposite: Be bent, and you will remain straight.
> Be vacant, and you will remain full. Be worn,
> and you will remain new. (*Tao Te Ching*, ch. 22)
>
> This is the way of life of the sage who has reached a higher point of view, a perspective from which the relative and polar relationships of all opposites are clearly perceived. These opposites include, first and foremost, the concepts of good and bad, which are interrelated in the same way as *yin* and *yang*. Recognizing the relativity of good and bad, and thus of all moral standards, *the Taoist sage does not strive for the good but rather tries to maintain a dynamic balance between good and bad.*[67] [emphasis added]

67. Fritjof Capra, *The Tao of Physics*, 2nd ed. (New York: Bantam Books, 1984), 103.

Or how about C.G. Jung's theory of evil as being but the fourth positive hypostasis of what he holds to be a Divine "Quaternity"? Of particular interest is the statement Jung makes at the end of the chapter on Christ in the text in which he introduces this bizarre blasphemy. As if summing up, he comments:

> The irreconcilable nature of the opposites in Christian psychology is due to their *moral accentuation*. This accentuation seems natural to us although, looked at historically, it is a legacy from the Old Testament with its emphasis on righteousness in the eyes of the law. *Such an influence is noticeably lacking in the East*, in the philosophical religions of India and China.[68] [emphasis added]

It is difficult to resist allowing Teilhard de Chardin to add his curious theory of evil to all this. It certainly hails from the same quarter of the mind:

> The problem of evil, that is to say, the reconciling of our failures, even the purely physical ones, with creative goodness and creative power, will always remain one of the most disturbing mysteries of the universe for both our hearts and our minds.[69] [Teilhard projects through his system the achievement of] a metaphysics of union, dominated by love in which even the Problem of Evil is given an acceptable intellectual solution (the statistical necessity of disorders within a multitude in process of organization).[70]
>
> Evil is inevitable in the course of a creation which develops within time. Here again the solution, which brings us freedom, is given us by evolution.[71]

Chesterton did not live to read these latter espousals of

68. C.G. Jung, *Psyche and Symbol*, "Aion" (London, 1958), 60; for theory of evil hypostasis, see same essay, 35ff.

69. Teilhard de Chardin, *The Divine Milieu* (New York: Harper Torchbooks, 1968), 85.

70. *Let Me Explain* (New York: Harper & Row, 1970), 146.

71. *How I Believe* (New York: Harper & Row, 1969), 89.

moral relativity, but one can imagine he would have written against them much the same critique as he writes on a following page of *Orthodoxy* about Friedrich Nietzsche:

> Nietzsche always escaped a question by a physical metaphor, like a cheery minor poet. He said, "beyond good and evil," because he had not the courage to say, "more good than good and evil," or "more evil than good and evil." Had he faced his thought without metaphors, he would have seen that it was nonsense.

Our author will assert in the next chapter that "a strict rule is not only necessary for ruling; it is also necessary for rebelling."

Any attempt to "enrich" reality by "integrating" evil into it will not make it more vibrant at all. It will suck the juice right out of the apple of temptation. Once again we witness the interconnection between the moral and speculative orders at the level of this inaugural choice. The full vigor and vibrancy of the good extremes is secured only by not embracing the evil partner of the bad extremes. This does not, however, mean ignoring or underrating the existence of decidedly evil agents. Already in Chesterton's schoolboy notebooks we find this remarkable paragraph, connecting the acknowledgement of morally bent agents with the full appreciation of what is truly good in reality:

> It may seem like a paradox, but there is nothing that depresses like pure optimism. For the attempt to think everything good must so lower the meaning of goodness as to make it at the end not much better than badness. By the time we have schooled ourselves to think measles as beautiful as health we are likely to have come to feel that health is as dreary as measles. The right way is the Christian way; to believe there is a positive evil somewhere and fight it: then everything else will be really jolly and pleasant: everything that is not against us will be for us. Roses will be

twice as red if you believe in the Devil. Skies will be twice as blue if you believe in the Devil.[72]

Just before turning to write *Orthodoxy*, Chesterton had finished his famous study of Charles Dickens. In that book we find the following digression which develops still further the idea that the bloodless optimism that fails to see the Devil finally fails to be optimistic:

> This optimism does exist—this optimism which is more hopeless than pessimism—this optimism which is the very heart of hell. Against such an aching vacuum of joyless approval there is only one antidote—a sudden and pugnacious belief in positive evil. This world can be made beautiful again by beholding it as a battlefield. When we have defined and isolated the evil thing, the colors come back into everything else. When evil things have become evil, good things, in a blazing apocalypse, become good. There are some men who are dreary because they do not believe in God; but there are many others who are dreary because they do not believe in the Devil. The grass grows green again when we believe in the Devil; the roses grow red again when we believe in the Devil. . . . For the full value of this life can only be got by fighting; the violent take it by storm. And if we have accepted everything, we have missed something—war. This life of ours is a very enjoyable fight, but a very miserable truce.[73]

Now in *Orthodoxy* Chesterton wishes to show that the full freedom of all those "parallel passions" toward which the human heart inclines can only be released and limbered when this terrible battle with moral evil and its emissaries is faced. "Granted the primary dogma of the war between divine and diabolic, the revolt and ruin of the world, their

72. Printed in *The Tablet*, April 4, 1953, 7.
73. CD, 287–88.

optimism and pessimism, as pure poetry, could be loosened like cataracts."

> By defining its main doctrine, the Church not only kept seemingly inconsistent things side by side, but, what was more, allowed them to break out in a sort of artistic violence otherwise possible only to the anarchists. Meekness grew more dramatic than madness.

We may now attempt to situate this new insight in the context of our two principles and three philosophical ideas. The first principle of cognition with which Chesterton began was the affirmation of the being of the world, in a grasp at once imprecise and yet incontestable, indefinable and yet unmistakable. The first principle of volition was the acceptance of a good to be done and an evil to be avoided. This too was obvious, but unexplainable. To the question, "Why should I do the good?", one could dig for no deeper reason than the reiterated assurance that it was indeed good.

Furthermore, just as the world became more and more marvelous and colorful to the man who did not try to reason his way to its existence (as did the maniac), so did the world yield more and more happiness to the man who did not try to decide for himself what is good (as did the Devil). We saw that the vitality of these two principles poises the mind to more readily discern the freedom, createdness and personal stamp in the world of our experience. Their three shadows—fatalism, monism and gnosticism—lie in wait for the mind unmoored from these principial anchors.

The new dimension brought to all this by Chapter 6 is that when these realities are more emphatically recognized by the mind, they are more emphatically recognized because their inherent *paradoxical* content is brought to the foreground of our perception. That this is true of the supernatural mysteries of Christianity is patent: God is three Persons in one Nature; Christ is God and man; the Eucharist is in its accidents, bread, and in its substance, Christ. But here as before,

Chesterton finds the Christian correspondence answering to a feature already well nested in the natural order. The universe *is* paradoxical.

If our author endeavors rhetorically to communicate this truth with images and comparisons that are at times wild and sportive, and if we feel ourselves unsteadied before a cosmos twirling with revolutions, I think a word of caution is in order. Paradox does not mean permanent peculiarity. The stunning oppositions it denotes are not inanities. It is Carroll's Wonderland that is intrinsically weird.

The White Queen really does live backwards behind the looking glass. But it is on *this* side of the looking-glass (and spending as little time before it as possible, I might add) that Chesterton has planted his feet. The paradoxes he points out, often in a personally playful and perhaps overwrought manner, exist in reality and are oppositions designed to sing in harmony. Only man and woman make a stable marriage. Love and war are both needed to settle a human heart in this life. Up and down are required for every bounce, and here and there for every trip. Negative and positive forces hold the atom together. And though the cosmos is revolutionary, the turns that make it so are as stable and reliable as the revolution of the earth around the sun. And even that recurrent cycle is but a reflection of reality's deepest surprise of all.

7. THE ETERNAL REVOLUTION

"There must be something eternal if there is to be anything sudden." In this chapter, Chesterton adds to the orthodox scenario yet another element which energizes and stabilizes at once. It is the fact that the rousing suddenness of a true revolution can draw its galvanizing impact only from the abiding stability of the center to which it returns. Otherwise, the awakening cry could turn into a lullaby.

The stationary goal, the fixed origin, the unchanging rule, the enduring model—so many ways of presuming a fixed point to which, or back to which, or according to which all progress, reformation and revolution must proceed if they are to mean anything at all. "We have said we must be fond of this world, even in order to change it. We now add that we must be fond of another world (real or imaginary) in order to have something to change it to."

> This, therefore, is our first requirement about the ideal toward which progress is directed; it must be fixed. Whistler used to make many rapid studies of a sitter; it did not matter if he tore up twenty portraits. But it would matter if he looked up twenty times, and each time saw a new person sitting placidly for his portrait.

This common-sense attestation was answered again by the Christian doctrine of Eden and the Fall, and the paradise to be regained. But the philosophical point is simply that all of our "*re*" words: *re*ligion, *re*formation, *re*naissance, *re*volution, *re*storation, *re*turn, etc., denote work that involves changing the world, and that any such change is possible only because of the unchanging norm, standing at the beginning, or better, at the principle of the things to be changed. Cognitive contact with that unchanging truth, before any supernatural *re*velation (there is another one!) enters the picture, is once again the very undeniability of the first evidences of the mind.

In a pre-rational conviction, the true and the good are known to exist. All the rational discourse that follows in exploring their instances and applications constitutes a kind of trek of the mind; it is a *dis*-course on its way through many lesser truths and abundant errors to an ultimate disclosure of the highest cause of being itself. All accomplishments of knowledge will still be measured by the unchanging principles of being in whose light they were made. The wild fun of toppling error and exposing stupidity will be directly proportionate to one's fidelity in *returning* to those principles each time they have been abandoned.

Now such a model or goal, whose existence and solidity we are now basing on the suggestive indices of first principles, must serve as model or goal for the very world and for us who inhabit it. The goodness all the world wants will be progressively unlocked only by the repeated capsizing of our lesser luxuries.

> The perfect happiness of men on earth (if it ever comes) will not be a flat and solid thing, like the satisfaction of animals. It will be an exact and perilous balance; like that of a desperate romance.

This was already ascertained in the previous chapter. Our needs are complex and more than mathematical, more than mammalian. The "hidden eccentricities of life" guessed by the Christian creed are likewise perceived by every normal man. There seems to be a deliberate inexactitude designed into our make-up, there for the sake of a larger harmony that transcends mere precision, and makes possible the wilder orders of beauty. In an equal-tempered harpsichord, all the notes but the octaves are slightly mistuned so that the player is free to modulate his harmonies over a sumptuous range of musical language. The more locally and scrupulously preened consonances of the older tuning dictated that the instruments kept their keys to a minimum.

The logic of the ideas moves once more to suspect the presence of a person: "Only a mind can place the exact proportions of a composite happiness." More than a tendency or a drift of nature, there is here a design and the orchestration of a mind. But this very complexity of design draws with it a concomitant peril once it is to any degree realized. Things fall apart. Chesterton's reflections on this send the ideas of "progressive," "conservative," and "liberal" into a free-for-all of mutual usurpation.

> [A]ll conservatism is based upon the idea that if you leave things alone you leave them as they are. But you do not. If you leave a thing alone you leave it to a torrent of change. If you leave a white post alone it will soon be a black post. If you particularly want it to be white you must be always painting it again; that is, you must be always having a revolution. Briefly, if you want the old white post you must have a new white post.

The three resulting "requirements for the ideal of progress" are that the ideal be: 1) fixed, 2) composite, and 3) in need of constant vigilance. Although the notion of creation occupies a conspicuous background to this chapter, it is to the other two ideas that the drive of the argument leads: person and freedom. Because of the fixed rule that makes any progress meaningful at all, one can exercise

> the liberty for which I chiefly care, the liberty to bind myself. Complete anarchy would not merely make it impossible to have any discipline or fidelity; it would also make it impossible to have any fun. To take an obvious instance, it would not be worthwhile to bet if a bet were not binding. The dissolution of all contracts would not only ruin morality but spoil sport. Now betting and such sports are only the stunted and twisted shapes of the original instinct of man for adventure and romance.... For the purpose even of the wildest romance results must be real; results must be irrevocable.

8. THE ROMANCE OF ORTHODOXY

As we examine this penultimate chapter of *Orthodoxy* and find Chesterton giving full reign to his deepest poetic instincts, it will be useful to brace ourselves firmly in the solid sobriety of the word that is the book's title. The final two chapters' reflections will not stray a step outside the severely cut delineation of the word's etymology: "right view." "Only the man with ordinary views is capable of having extraordinary visions."[74] Nothing could better characterize G.K. Chesterton's philosophical message than the assertion that the right view of reality is, in the last analysis, the ordinary view, and that it is of the very nature of the ordinary view to foster romantic visions. That this has little to do with sighs and gasps and aching hearts should be evident shortly.

At the end of "The Paradoxes of Christianity," Chesterton maintained "there never was anything so perilous or so exciting as orthodoxy," for "to be sane is more dramatic than to be mad. It was the equilibrium of a man behind madly rushing horses, seeming to stoop this way and to sway that, yet in every attitude having the grace of statuary and the accuracy of arithmetic." The present chapter unleashes a whole ballet of emancipated consequences, leaping forth, as it were, at the declaration of that one discovery.

But here again, the ever-present menace typified by the maniac and the skeptic must first be sundered off by the terrible swift sword of the will. As we learned two chapters ago, the fun of all the good polarities is secured by picking sides in this moral polarity. In this chapter, Chesterton warns us against the contradictions of those who flaunt new and modern "freedoms":

> It means freeing that peculiar set of dogmas loosely called scientific, dogmas of monism, of pantheism, or of Arianism, or of necessity. And every one of these (and we will take them one by one) can be shown to be the natural ally of oppression.

Chesterton is inching his way up to what he sees as a final confrontation between East and West. All the issues of the book have been dancing at the skirts of this simmering

74. FF, vii.

enmity. As he moves closer, he makes one identification of capital importance.

Our author first observes the common enthusiasm among academics of his day for pointing out "that Christianity and Buddhism are very much alike, especially Buddhism." As with his earlier adherence to skepticism, Chesterton shared this view until someone laid out to him the reasons for supporting it. In fact, most of these modern truisms sound plausible until someone finally explains the reasons behind them. Then you are dissuaded. So it was that our author found his way back to orthodox theology partly with the help of the "heretics."

> It was Huxley and Herbert Spencer and Bradlaugh who brought me back. . . . They sowed in my mind my first wild doubts of doubt. . . . The rationalist made me question whether reason was of any use whatever, and when I had finished Herbert Spencer I had got as far as doubting (for the first time) whether evolution had occurred at all. As I laid down the last of Colonel Ingersoll's atheistic lectures the dreadful thought broke across my mind, "Almost thou persuadest me to be a Christian." I was in a desperate way.

Especially those who equated Christianity and Buddhism were trying to stretch a deceptive membrane over the deepest intellectual chasm ever opened before the human mind.

> All humanity does agree that we are in a net of sin. Most of humanity agrees that there is some way out. But as to what is the way out, I do not think that there are two institutions in the universe which contradict each other so flatly as Buddhism and Christianity.

What had set off the first series of doubts of religious relativism were the respective artistic productions of East and West. Chesterton had of course begun as an artist himself. "The Buddhist saint always had his eyes shut, while the Christian saint always had them very wide open. . . . The

Buddhist is looking with a peculiar intentness inwards. The Christian is staring with a frantic intentness outwards. If we follow that clue steadily we shall find some interesting things."

It should be pointed out in passing, that our author's critique of the "inward" emphasis of the East and much modern philosophy needs some careful qualification to clear it of the charge of an all-too-worldly Christian spirituality. I do not know of a text where Chesterton addresses this potential confusion. He hardly treats of mysticism in the stricter sense anyway. In a private conversation in 1930, he confessed that the anti-Catholic prejudice he faced during his career was such that he "had no time or opportunity to write about the Catholic mystics. The writers of his generation, he [Chesterton] said, were like soldiers defending the city. There was no opportunity of knowing the treasures inside the gates."[75] Since he turned so rarely to these questions, he seems never to have bothered with the pertinent distinction.

The point this chapter wishes to make is that the Christian mystic wants to know and love someone *other* than himself, namely God and his fellow-creatures. He does not wish merely to know himself, and certainly not to know that he himself *is* God and everything else. This last Chesterton holds, however unfairly, to be the error of the Eastern mystic in his most ultimate and evolved form. The contrast with the Christian ideal is so complete and the confusion of the two such an enormity of culpable intellectual blindness, Chesterton goes to great lengths to dramatically contrast the outward eyes of the Christian saint against the inward eyes of the Buddha and his followers.

Now the important qualification that needs to be urged is simply that the Christian also fosters an inner, indeed, an

75. Reminiscence of Fr. Malachy Lynch from 1960, printed in *Universe* (June 27, 1986), 23.

inward life. St. Francis could also be found closing his eyes and looking within. Perhaps it is the difference in what he then looked at and what the Buddha looks at, that confirms the substance of Chesterton's radical contrast. St. Francis's inward glance is not looking at St. Francis, or at nothing; it is looking within-without—that is to say, he is looking with his interior, spiritual face inwardly at the spiritual world of God, His angels and saints. And that is a world which is distinct from St. Francis, although, through the grace of God, it comes to dwell more and more within him.

That interior world is real, just as the outer physical world is real; indeed, it has a consistency and "solidity" of its own, because it is unchanging and anchored permanently in the reality of God. Both the outer and the inner worlds are therefore very real worlds we are related to, and the point at issue is simply that this reality is other than the person beholding it, and is best depicted by the eyes of the saint riveted in an outward gaze. We must merely remember, as an important corrective: that gaze stands also for the invisible, inward contemplation performed by interior, equally fiery eyes, looking upon an even vaster landscape of distinct realities.

I have highlighted the stark profile of every choice in the Chestertonian defense of freedom: a "yes" to one course of events along with a million "no's" to all the others. The most crucial of choices, that of good over evil, turns out to be the trail-blazing act that opens to the mind's eye all the animation and adventure a person could desire. We have also seen that the most unique choice of all was the choice of the universe itself, made by its Maker from among so many possible worlds.

Moving now from the concepts of "freedom" and "creation" to the third pivotal concept of person, we find that here too a basic separation is presupposed. The "something personal in the world" our author had noted earlier would hardly be accounted for, were it not a message or intention of some sort from at least one person to at least one other. But as much as upon the other two concepts, Chesterton thought that the East had thrown its mists over this one too. How often are Western orientalizers (to be distinguished from orientalists, a more legitimate calling) heard uttering

> the doctrine that we are really all one person; that there are no real walls of individuality between man and man. If I may put it so, she does not tell us to love our neighbors; she tells us to *be* our neighbours.

To this, Chesterton sharply rejoins: "I never heard any suggestion in my life with which I more violently disagree."

> I want to love my neighbour not because he is I, but precisely because he is not I. I want to adore the world, not as one likes a looking-glass, because it is one's self, but as one loves a woman, because she is entirely different. If souls are separate love is possible, if souls are united love is obviously impossible. A man may be said loosely to love himself, but he can hardly fall in love with himself, or, if he does, it must be a monotonous courtship. If the world is full of real selves, they can be really unselfish selves. . . . It is just here that Buddhism is on the side of modern pantheism and immanence. And it is just here that Christianity is on the side of humanity and liberty and love.

It is nearly hopeless to try to summarize or paraphrase the next pages without losing precisely the succinct economy of phrase which makes Chesterton's insights so piercing.

The watchword of Oriental ontology is for Chesterton, look wherever you wish, "unity." And the unity meant is precisely *ontological* unity. For the Easterner so conceived, all separation, division and opposition are, in the last analysis, so many fissures in the face of reality, to be overcome by being erased—or, better, by "realizing" that they are not really there after all. The best of Western ontology, on the other hand (the very other hand), proclaims discernment, distinction, fruitful opposition, and, most loudly, relationship, as woven into the very fabric of being.

> The Christian saint is happy because he has verily been cut off from the world; he is separate from things and is staring at them in astonishment. But why should the Buddhist saint be astonished at things?—since there is really only one thing, and that being impersonal can hardly be astonished at itself. There have been many pantheist poems suggesting wonder, but no really successful one. The pantheist cannot wonder, for he cannot praise God or praise anything as really distinct from himself.

In these pages, a cascade of insights is poured unsorted over our mind. Let us at least isolate one crucial corollary that is drawn here.

> There is no real possibility of getting out of pantheism any special impulse to moral action. For pantheism implies in its nature that one thing is as good as another; whereas action implies in its nature that one thing is greatly preferable to another.... The truth is that the western energy that dethrones tyrants has been directly due to the Western theology that says, "I am I, thou art thou."
>
> The Indian saint may reasonably shut his eyes because he is looking at that which is I and Thou and We and They and It.... That external vigilance which has always been the mark of Christianity (the command that we should watch and pray) has expressed itself both in typical Western orthodoxy and in typical Western politics: but both depend on the idea of a divinity transcendent, different from ourselves, a deity that disappears.

The full social, economic and political consequences of this allegedly Eastern view as against the Western philosophical principles are matters about which Chesterton was to write some of his best books, such as *What's Wrong with the World* and *The Outline of Sanity*. An additional book would be required to show exactly how pertinent the notions of freedom, creation and person turn out to be in the defense of the institutions of the state, the family and private property respectively.

The Christian doctrine of the Trinity is shown to be one that answers to this feature of division and distinction, which is found to lie so deep in the make-up of reality. As a pure supernatural mystery, the West of course did not think it up on its own; still, it does finally correspond to the perceived world and the impulses of the heart. As Chesterton says of the Trinitarian doctrine: "this thing that bewilders the intellect utterly quiets the heart."

The separation of persons in the created order proves to be a reflection of the distinction of Persons in the divine order. But we need not appeal to the revealed truth to see that they are separate. Our common sense will suffice. The great dogma just caps the conviction with an unexpected epiphany of its purpose. That is to say, we are separate ontologically in order to be reunited; not, however, in a blend, but instead, in an embrace. The whole doctrine of love in the West is one ardent insistence that this intended intimacy of charity is not just "oneness." As a choice, love presupposes the diversity of the one chosen from the lover, excluding the millions not chosen. It is a oneness of will which reaches out for a oneness of being of a special kind, the kind we call "communion." Here once more, as so often in Chesterton's writing, we have a whole flurry of concepts buzzing at once. Let us attempt another provisional orchestration:

Orthodoxy is a romance because the ultimate "opposition" in reality is the paradox of love. "God is love" is not just a flowery consolation or a story-book strategy pandering to our sentimental illusions in wrestling with the Absolute. It is a hard ontological fact. Western thought has been peculiarly charged with the mystery of love ever since Christian philosophy became a possible form of reflection. Anyone comparing Eastern and Western mysticism (the latter particularly in the Catholic tradition) must sooner or later be struck by a difference so radical it may easily masquerade as an identity. Just as when the temperature gets far enough below zero, one can have the illusion of getting warm again, likewise here.

> It is a great mistake to suppose that love unites and unifies men. Love diversifies them, because love is directed towards individuality.[76]
>
> You cannot love a thing without wanting to fight for it. You cannot fight without something to fight for. To love a thing without wishing to fight for it is not to love at all; it is lust. . . . Wherever human nature is human and unspoilt by any special sophistry, there exists this natural kinship between war and wooing, and that natural kinship is called romance.[77]

Love and war are the two expressions on the one face of romance. In this life, the latter expression is inevitable, and all the more so, the more you desire the first. The yogi of the East desires neither, for love is personal; it is free; it is creative. And all three of our Christian philosophical concepts are at home in love, and all three of their denials result at last in producing an apersonal, incarcerating and monistic union, where finally there is nothing to fight about anyway.

Romance, in other words, is dangerous. Your heart will be broken, but it turns out to be the only way in this life that it can truly be opened. This built-in challenge is the peril fled by the yogi and embraced by the Christian. It makes all the difference between a cycle and a story, a pattern and a picture, the turning of a wheel and the turning of a bend in the road.

> To say that all will be well anyhow is a comprehensible remark: but it cannot be called the blast of a trumpet. Europe ought rather to emphasize possible perdition; and

76. CD, 254.
77. ACD, 28.

> Europe always has emphasized it. Here its highest religion is at one with all its cheapest romances. To the Buddhist or the Eastern fatalist existence is a science or a plan which must end up in a certain way. But to a Christian existence is a story, which may end up in any way. . . . But the point is that a story is exciting because it has in it so strong an element of will, of what theology calls free will. You cannot finish a sum how you like. But you can finish a story how you like.

The romance of love involves a plurality of persons possessed of free wills, and liable to do anything. When the mechanism of Fate is dethroned in the Christian universe, man senses his freedom and begins to tremble. In order that freedom may be fully free, and coexist at last with peace, man must be free at last of freedom's mocker, license. Lest adventure become calamity, man longs to have his freedom crowned and consummated by authority. But he must seek, and he must ask. The Author of freedom knows this well, and waits, knowing this too to be a consequence of creation—for in creating the world, God did not just put it there, but in a very real sense turned it loose.

9. AUTHORITY AND THE ADVENTURER

In this final chapter, Chesterton inventories his many discoveries, and then voices a question: Would it not be possible to hold on to these new lights and dismiss their Christian correspondences? In recapitulating the truths, independent as they are from any absolute reliance on Christian doctrine, he wonders if capitulation to the secularist might still be feasible. Or in the words of his own *advocatus diaboli*: "If you see clearly the kernel of common sense in the nut of Christian orthodoxy, why cannot you simply take the kernel and leave the nut? This is the real question, this is the last question" says our author. And since it addresses the angle of our interpretation head-on, Chesterton's answer to it will be the best concluding commentary on the relation of common sense to Christian revelation.

To begin with, we have at last an unambiguous denial that this book was intended to be one of ordinary Christian apologetics; insisting "I am a rationalist," he goes on: "I should be glad to meet at any other time the enemies of an account of my own growth in spiritual certainty." His first discovery was common sense, not the Incarnation. His second discovery was that of "having found the moral atmosphere of the Incarnation to be common sense."

The arguments against the faith showed themselves upon examination to be "common nonsense." It is due to this approach of our author that we could claim at the outset that this book is basically philosophical and not theological. But now he makes the third discovery that without the fostering ambience of Christianity, even the natural truths become strangely elusive. The natural seems unable even to be natural without the supernatural. And even the worldly adventure may well lose its natural thrill without a supernatural authority to protect it.

To frame this last insight, Chesterton first offers to summarize his arguments, as promised. He does so, however, by way of further illustrations. The main argument rests after all on "an enormous accumulation of small but unanimous facts." We will take as sample of his examples only the first three.

Simply opening his eyes, our author sees three bald facts:

1) Man is clearly a radically and stunningly different sort of being from all the beasts he shares oxygen and water with.

2) All the traditions of the world speak of some distant past happiness, or golden age, from which we have, for whatever reason, receded.

3) The countries of Europe that have the strongest linkage with Catholic clergy and custom, also have the most colorful dress, the most rigorous dances and the most sumptuous banquets.

Chesterton is understandably bewildered by the placid denial of all three of these facts by a host of high-brow faces looking up from a battery of modern books. And then, turning from these unruffled visages to the pulpits of Christendom, he hears the oracles of supernatural revelation heartily seconding his observations. Not only that, they offer an explanation for all three facts:

> the theory that twice was the natural order interrupted by some explosion or revelation such as people now call "psychic." Once Heaven came upon the earth with a power or a seal called the image of God, whereby man took command of Nature; and once again (when in empire after empire men had been found wanting) Heaven came to save mankind in the awful shape of a man. This would explain why the mass of men always look backwards; and why the only corner where they in any sense look forwards is the little continent where Christ has His Church.

The next few paragraphs take us through additional examples of simple ascertainments about Christianity being irrationally contradicted by minds looking through books rather than through eyes. But Chesterton gives these examples as specimens of that "accumulation of varied facts" pointing to the faith. "But among these millions of facts all flowing one way there is, of course, one question sufficiently solid and separate to be treated briefly, but by itself; I mean the objective occurrence of the supernatural." Believing miracles turns out to be as common-sensical an attestation as "believing an old apple-woman when she bears testimony to a murder."

It rests on the acceptance, once again, of a principle of authority outside oneself, for which the mind has already been disposed by its initial acceptance of the indemonstrable first evidences. The very "miracle" of creation itself, this unnecessary gift of being, deducible from no a priori axiom, and at best only the arduously arguable causality to which a metaphysical resolution can lead—this central idea, and the notion of person and freedom so interwoven with it, assume the sort of stability in one's mental make-up ordinarily reserved for first principles:

> [My] own positive conviction that personal creation is more conceivable than material fate, is, I admit, in a sense, un-discussible. I will not call it a faith or an intuition, for those words are mixed up with mere emotion, it is strictly an intellectual conviction; but it is a primary intellectual conviction like the certainty of self or the good of living.

In the final pages of *Orthodoxy*, Chesterton insists that both the authority of the senses in common-sense discernments, and the authority of Christianity in its central dogmas, are of the primary, inarguable sort. About this latter authority, our author will have an increasing fund of commentary in his later works, as the earthly domicile of this dominion urges itself more and more upon his mind. At the beginning of the book, he had deliberately prescinded from discussing "the very fascinating but quite different question of what is the present seat of authority for the proclamation of that creed." If Chesterton had ever revised this first edition of *Orthodoxy*—something he never systematically did with any of his books—I fancy he would have changed nothing at all in the book except the two words in that sentence: "quite different." We shall see why in an instant.

Our author had discovered at the beginning of the book that "man can understand everything by the help of what he does not understand," speaking of the mind's first bow to the evidence of the existence of the world. He now discovers in Christianity that "something that we have never in any full sense known [God], is not only better than ourselves, but even more natural to us than ourselves."

He had discovered in the natural moral order that "all the dizzy and colossal things conceded depend upon one small thing withheld. All the wild and whirling things that are let loose depend upon one thing that is forbidden." He now discovers that "the outer ring of Christianity is a rigid guard of ethical abnegations and professional priests; but inside that inhuman guard you will find the old human life dancing like children, and drinking wine like men. For Christianity is the only frame for pagan freedom." That supposedly "quite different" issue of the seat of Christ's authority on earth Chesterton came to see as not quite so different after all. That authority turned out to be as palpable and as visible as the "impossible universe that stares us in the face." Now in the man G.K. Chesterton, the certain "something that we have never in any full sense known" was already more natural to him than he fully knew when he penned those lines. It dawned powerfully upon him in the years that ensued.

The key of the senses and the key of Christ were seen to open their respective gates: one, the free creation, and the other, the Creator's free Church, but both as bridges to the New Jerusalem. In the nine chapters of *Orthodoxy*, the ordinary view of the world and its challenge points an excited finger at an extraordinary vision of the Church of Christ. But guided by the mind of an impassioned lover of wisdom, it is the finger of philosophy that points, and it is the human hunger for reality that excites.

IV
The Poise of the Western Mind

You can only find truth with logic if you have already found truth without it.

~ G.K.C.[1]

Chesterton's work brings to my mind three salient convictions that must inform any philosophical stance that can begin, and remain, in full contact with reality: 1) acceptance of the sovereign transcendence of the universe over our consciousness and the capital importance of acknowledging it; 2) the natural but subordinate role of reason in human affairs, and the danger of it transgressing its limits; and 3) the recognition of our thought as constitutionally situated in an ambience of first principles, long before the discernments of philosophy can safely develop. The fourth and concluding part of this book will attempt to briefly outline each of these convictions.

1. OUR USELESS UNIVERSE

Poetry, philosophy and prayer have something in common. Beneath the obvious distinction between their separate acts lie three common traits that make their authentic practi-

1. *Illustrated London News*, March 15, 1919.

tioners into spiritual brethren. The first regards their end. All three are human aspirations to a certain good which is considered to be an end in itself, transcending the sphere of immediate utility. They have to do with the kinds of activities that you could keep on doing forever.

An eternal labor would be something like hell, but an eternal volleyball game would only be slightly better. Even the fun of sports serves the end of winning, or of relaxation, and once that end is served, boredom lies in wait. But if only our tongue could take it, a never-ending poem on an undying theme could hold our interest forever, strophe upon strophe being added, and delight never abating. Likewise, an eternal contemplation of the truth could, if the Truth were eternal, keep us everlastingly entertained. Finally, the prayer of praise, again presupposing an infinite Object of praise, could also go on forever with no hint of weariness.

To be sure, the poet may recite a poem in order to settle his spirit, but would his spirit be truly settled if the poem did not succeed in lifting his eye to something beyond that transient gratification? Likewise, the philosopher may speculate to answer a pressing question, and the man of prayer engage in the prayer of petition to meet a present need—but neither will the philosophy shed light nor the prayer summon an answer, unless both are unconstrained by an overriding functional design. They must be essentially free, even in order to be accidentally useful.

The poet sings or versifies for the sake of the very grasp of being embodied in the poem (or in the song, the symphony or the story). And although the etymology of the word "prayer" points first to petition, even that petition must be of a piece with a larger end if its supplications are to be heard; that is to say, they too must be a selfless acknowledgment of the power, transcendence and goodness of God. *All* true prayer is, in the final analysis, praise.

But what do I mean by claiming that philosophy must be

regarded as free of ultimate utility, something that is pursued finally for its own sake? We must address this question precisely because of the influence our modern thinkers have had on our notion of philosophy. Only by establishing this intrinsic freedom of philosophy can the Chestertonian defense of our first encounter with the universe be fully appreciated.

The yoking of philosophical thought to a this-worldly utility was ventured by Descartes "to reach knowledge that will be of much utility in this life.... Instead of the speculative philosophy now taught in the schools we can find a practical one," learning how bodies work and how we can employ them, "and so make ourselves masters and possessors of nature."[2] This spirit predominates in the minds of Descartes and his epigones. The hitherto reigning Aristotelian ethos, according to which "that which is desirable on its own account and for the sake of knowing it, is more of the nature of Wisdom than that which is desirable on account of its results,"[3] and that "all the sciences, indeed, are more necessary than this [metaphysics], but none is better,"[4] had already been held up to scorn by Francis Bacon.

Bacon compared such self-sufficing speculation with a sterile whore, whereas the fruitful inventiveness of the new science was like a fruitful mother. Only God and the angels are entitled to be mere "spectators"; the rest of us have to work. The purpose of true knowledge for Bacon is "to enrich human life with new inventions and new riches."[5] In the Latin edition, he even offers us an almost scholastic saw: "*Quod in operando utilissimum, id in scientia verissimum*"

2. René Descartes, *Discourse on Method and Meditations*, trans. by Laurence Lafleur (New York: Library of Liberal Arts, 1960), 45.

3. Aristotle, *Metaphysics*, I, 2, 982a 15–18, trans. by W. D. Ross.

4. Ibid., a 10–11.

5. *De Dignitate et Augmentis Scientiarum*, I; VII, 1.

(Whatever is most useful in operation, is most true in science).[6]

Bacon sums up the new attitude best in his grim injunction: "Nature ought to be put to the rack, to compel it to answer our questions." All this will be repeated not only by Descartes, but also by Locke, who insists that "there is no knowledge worthy of the name excepting those which lead to some new or useful invention"; by Diderot, who insists that man must "torment nature into giving up her secrets."[7] Kant of course used a telling quote from Bacon's *Magna Instauratio* as epigraph for his *Critique of Pure Reason*, including the key phrase, "I am laboring to lay the foundation, not of any sect or doctrine, but of human utility and power."[8] Right at the beginning of his *Critique,* Kant compares the old-fashioned natural philosopher to a pupil, listening attentively to *all* that his teacher (nature) is telling him; the modern scientist, in contrast, he compares to a judge (or we might add, the prosecutor) in a court of law, insisting the intimidated witness in the dock (nature again) *only* answer the questions put and otherwise keep quiet.

Now it was not until the early 19th century that the two terms "philosophy" and "science" came to be conventionally distinguished. One must keep that in mind while reading the above statements. Philosophy had tried desperately ever since Bacon to claim its territorial rights in the world of knowledge, having looked on rather hopelessly as one domain after another was staked out and fenced off by the new scientific methods. Only the human soul, the world as a whole, and God Himself seemed to evade these new yardsticks. The more avant-garde among the new thinkers began

6. *Novum Organum*, I, 82.

7. All three quotes cited in John Emmet Hughes, *The Church and the Liberal Society* (Princeton, NJ: Princeton University Press, 1944), 64–65.

8. Bacon, *Essays, Advancement of Learning, New Atlantis and Other Pieces*, ed. R. F. Jones (New York, 1937), 251.

to ask if maybe these "metaphysical objects" dodged the new measures for the simple reason that they did not exist. We saw, after all, in what a faded version of their former selves Kant had left these three residual domains of inquiry.

Before briefly recalling the new beginnings of the post-Kantian mind, which, to a large extent, broke free for a spell from the mechanistic model, one remark should be made about the pre-Kantian miscarriages. For the greater part, they aspired to imitate the New Science; and that meant making philosophy a means to practical ends. There was as yet little reason to distinguish between philosophy and the New Science. Pining for a wisdom that would be rich in practical fruit, philosophers labored to dodge the Baconian lampoon directed at all the unfashionable scholastics, who "out of no great quantity of matter, and infinite agitation of wit, spin out unto us those laborious webs of learning which are extant in their books . . . but of no substance or profit."[9] They tried to make philosophy too into a strict science after the new vogue, and that meant mathematical exactitude as the guiding star. But turned into a servant, she proved herself awkward and in the way, inclined to vague, time-consuming reflections on forms and ultimate causes. Kant's *Critique* appeared to be a cruel, but wholesome purge of this pathetically self-abasing exercise.

After all this, the Idealists had their flash of glory, went under, and then re-surfaced again and again in the new universe of subjectivity offered to the post-Kantian philosopher. Against the love/hate background chorus of the Romantics, Hegel and his fellows hoisted the term "philosophy" onto its own proper mast, and sailed off wistfully into the transcendental subject. The little boats of the scientists they left to pursue their separate stars. Nonetheless, this new emancipation of philosophy from the sciences was to have a mixed

9. Ibid., 212.

fortune. Marx, as we know, turned the Hegelian world onto its head precisely to make it *do* something. And at the same time he insisted on making his philosophy truly scientific. Philosophers had hitherto *interpreted* the world, he complained, but the real point of philosophy was to *change* the world. (*Theses on Feuerbach*, n.11)

Even the subjective world, as we have already said, began to fall under the searchlights of the new psychology, and knowledge of it prove quite useful too. So it did not take long for many philosophers to turn again to the sciences, which had indeed taken several interesting turns in the 19th and 20th centuries. Once again, many philosophers tried to take their cues from them. This is particularly true in positivism, analytic philosophy and phenomenology. Husserl entitled one of his seminal works "Philosophy as a Strict Science," and endeavored to make his method and his subject matter "strictly scientific." We have seen where that led Husserl.

The basic mistake in all of this, Chesterton would claim, lies in refusing to start philosophical thought with the world as a whole—a big, imprecise and unmanageable whole, but a supremely evident one. That initial object of philosophical reflection can never be made into a means. *You cannot use the universe.* However, one of the privileges of being endowed with a spiritual soul is that you can do something far better than use it—you can notice it. As Josef Pieper writes:

> That is the tradition of Western philosophy: to have spirit, or to be spirit, means to exist in the midst of the whole of reality and before the whole of being; *vis-à-vis de l'univers*, Spirit does not exist in "a" world, nor in "its" world, but in "the" world in the sense of *visibilia omnia et invisibilia*.[10]

10. Josef Pieper, *Leisure: The Basis of Culture*, trans. by Alexander Dru (New York: Mentor, 1963), 88.

2. REASON: THE HANDMAID OF WONDER

The second common denominator between poetry, philosophy and prayer is that all three have to do with the marvelous. Not with the curious, but with the marvelous. I am willing to listen to a nuclear physicist or a molecular biologist express his amazement at the phenomena he studies. There are wonders of nature, and the scientist—whether through microscope or telescope—is entitled to marvel at them. But to the extent that he achieves genuine amazement, the spirit of philosophy has impinged upon his science. Modern science, in virtue of its own techniques and inspired by its forced marriage with technology, tends to be far more in the service of curiosity and power than of true wonder. Curiosity invites us to tamper; wonder summons us to contemplation.

In modern parlance, curiosity has become more or less equated with the "*desiderium sciendi*" (the desire to know) of which, in scholastic philosophy, it was the excess. Even so, we can shift it back into its negative sense by urging that someone "not be so curious." We clearly mean, in such a case, that they should keep their noses out of things that are none of their business. Thus, even the word's more countenanced meaning is interconnected with this less honorable connotation. It is significant that St. Thomas Aquinas, who carefully delineates the proper grounds of the "desire to know," and analyses "*curiositas*" as a vice,[11] at the same time offers high praises for the reaction of wonder. Obviously, he sees curiosity and wonder as two quite different responses to potential knowledge. Our modern world, with all its intriguing gadgetry, can easily lose sight of this distinction.

Even in the more customary construal of curiosity, in which it may be loosely equated with wonder, we are in the

11. *Summa Theologiae*, II-IIae, q. 167.

face of something different from Thomas's *admiratio* (his Latin for wonder, meaning much more than our "admiration"). The curious reader of today reads to find the answer to a question or the solution to a problem, and is inquisitive and relentless in tracking them down. Once he has his prey, though, the curiosity, the "wonder," ceases. Now he knows. Old Pythagoras, when once asked what the fruit of all his thought would be, replied: *mede thaumazein* (to marvel at nothing). This is one side, but only one side, of the human pursuit of intellectual light.

In Aristotle, this interpretation was also very present, though the deeper sense of wonder was close to the surface. He maintains that "it is owing to their wonder that men both now begin and at first began to philosophize; they wondered originally at the obvious difficulties, then advanced little by little and stated difficulties about the greater matters."[12] He speaks elsewhere, however, of a wonder which partakes directly of a kind of pleasure and happiness,[13] thus suggesting it may be related to something terminal, beyond the temporary condition of someone not yet "in the know." In the final analysis, a host of epistemological questions are associated with the nature of wonder.[14] What is important for us in relation to Chesterton is that St. Thomas picked up on the Aristotelian theme of wonder, and, integrating it with the related themes of contemplation and the beatific vision, was able to eye a content quite beyond modern curiosity, and habitually forgotten by most of us today. It is this content that Chesterton reminds us of.

In a passing remark, Aristotle compares "the lover of myth" with the "lover of wisdom" (i.e., the philosopher), for

12. *Metaphysics*, I, 2, 982b 12–15.

13. *Rhetoric*, II, 1371a 31–34; *Nichomachean Ethics*, 10, 7, 1177a 25.

14. See, for instance, André Guindon, "l'emerveillement," in *Eglise et Théologie*, 7, 1976, 61–97.

both have to do with "wonder."[15] It is used by Thomas more than once as a compact commentary on the interrelatedness of the poetic, the philosophic, and the mystical.[16] Here I shall merely summarize the content of his teaching as it bears upon our topic.

Wonder is our human response to an effect whose cause is hidden from our mind. Since this response can occur in very different ways, the concept of wonder turns out to be analogical. In the more usual sense, we speak of wondering *about the cause.* "Who made the world?" "Why does the camel have a hump?" "How come the sun is red when it sets?" If the effect is also a great and imposing phenomenon—as is for example the world itself—one may also wonder *at the effect.* In both cases one is responding with the will to an intellectually ascertained ignorance. The magic of wonder lies in a thing being grasped as simultaneously known and unknown. If the hidden cause is the focus of the wonder, then because it is hidden. If the obvious effect is the focus, then because it is obviously a remarkable effect, and probably of a still more remarkable cause. This interwoven tapestry of knowledge and ignorance at once spurs and spurns the mind.

Man's natural desire to know is a fruit of the will's natural inclination to the good. The truth being simply the good of the intellect, the will desires it. *Bonum est agendum, malum vitandum* (the good is to be done; evil, avoided). The converse evil fled or fought by the will is, in the case of the intellect, ignorance, whether in the vicious form of falsehood or in the merely neutral form of ignorance. (The scholastics would complete the distinctions by making the last word

15. *Metaphysics*, loc. cit., 982b 19.

16. St. Thomas Aquinas, *In Metaphysicam*, l. 3, n.55; for supernatural connection see *In Job*, c.41, 1.2; *Contra Gentiles*, II, c.2 and III, c.62; *Summa Theol.*, II-II, qu.19, art.11 and qu.180, art.3, 3m.

read "nescience," ignorance being reserved for not knowing something you *should* know.)

Now in the case of wonder, the will encounters in the wonderful object both the present evil of ignorance, and the potential future evil of falsehood. This last is a peril because of the intellect's natural penchant for judgment as its native means of securing knowledge. The natural desire to know inclines the intellect to make judgments, to "bite into" its knowledge, as it were. In the face of ignorance, the virtuous will reacts to this possible evil of false judgment by withholding judgment, and furthermore by seeking to overcome that evil by pursuing additional knowledge.

The richness and mystery of the response of wonder has made it helpful to specify it with concepts borrowed from similar responses in the sensory appetites. For these last, an impending future evil of difficult elimination evokes the emotion of fear. Likewise, the possible acquisition of a difficult future good, evokes the emotion of hope. Thus seen in the context of the will's natural desire for the good of the intellect, which is truth, one can speak analogously of wonder as being a kind of fear generative of a kind of hope.

In poetry and the arts, one begins with a simple delight in the exercise of the senses, particularly the interior sense of the imagination. The very exercise of these first knowing powers, as Aristotle teaches us, brings pleasure.[17] But the more this first mode of knowledge grows, the greater becomes the realization of how much more one does *not* know. This *docta ignorantia* (learned ignorance) regards not only all the additional things one has not yet experienced, but also, and more profoundly, the very things one thinks one already knows. They turn out to bear unplumbed mysteries hitherto unsuspected. Poetry, of course, had already allowed the mystery of being to come to light. It did not,

17. *Metaphysics*, I, 1.

however, give us a resolution of the mystery, or even try to. This is because poetry begins with delight, but—if it is good poetry—ends in wonder.

It is philosophy that truly begins in wonder. But this is no longer the merely curious wonder at an observed phenomenon whose behavioral laws one seeks to describe. This concern with the "how" is interesting and at times imperative, but its answers are such that they typically lay wonder to rest. One may admire the order and regularity of the Newtonian cosmos, but you really have no need of further wonder, so long at least as you stay within the framework of the mechanist's questions. If you begin instead asking things like: "But what *is* gravity, anyway?", or, "Whence does this cosmic order come, to begin with?", or quite simply, "What does it all mean?", you will find yourself settling down into a chair and beginning a long and maybe never-ending meditation. Bacon will be furious, because you have taken up the "sterile" business of traditional philosophizing. You will probably have little time left over to make steam-engines or plan lunar expeditions. Should plans for embarking upon such projects steal into your mind, one of your philosophical questions might promptly take the wind out of their sails: "But why?"

Few people in the ancient and few in the medieval world made machines. There seem to have been a few medieval Muslims who tinkered with mechanical technology and even the possibility of internal combustion engines (they weren't entirely ignorant of the oil under their feet), but when they did so, we note with a smile, it was only to make toys for entertainment (much like the traditional Chinese use of gunpowder more for fireworks, than for guns). This is a complex topic, and I am not (nor was Chesterton) advocating a Luddite solution to technological excess. I should like, however, to defend pre-modern simplicity in the area of technology as not always deriving from mere stupidity, or from an atavistic inability to make gears and burn petroleum. There could be another reason why they did not become industrialized. It could really be that they simply chose not to. A sustaining ethos of wonder can make a man at least hesitate before reaching out to tamper with nature and manipulate the universe.

Now, we have already established that wonder is a kind of fear. The Scriptures say that "the fear of God is the beginning of [supernatural] wisdom." (Prov. 1, 1) The fear of the universe, I submit, is the beginning of natural wisdom. Even today, we are still so ignorant of it, and all of our so-vaunted knowledge is striped through with precious veins of marvelous unknowing. Physicists tell us that some 95% of material reality is made of "dark" matter and energy, which basically means they don't really know what it is. The child, and with him the common man, are still full of this respectable fear before the unknown. As a consequence of this fear, the universe deserves being both wondered at and wondered about. The plethora of physical and mechanical details we have hitherto mastered tell us *how* it runs, from Archimedes all the way down to particle physics. But this will never be able to compete with the simple sensory intake of a human being face to face with the expanse of the sky and all the world beneath it.

The universe—whether its marvelous Maker is prayed to, its songs sung, or its spectacles and causes pondered—will, for us wonderstruck thinkers, remain well beyond the sphere of utility. Something other than expedience will fuel our questions. And before one day being permitted to see the Face of the God we pray to, we will first try and learn to see the face of the universe we live in. This is a lesson we all are in need of relearning. In our present jaded state, once the sensory witness of that world has been humbly embraced, we turn to poetry and the arts to prime us for a life of amazement. One might put it like this: in order to seize upon an idea philosophically, we must first be seized by an image poetically. Only after enjoying such a vision of the very universe around us, can philosophy truly begin. One of Chesterton's characters got seized by the fact:

> "Listen to me," cried Syme with extraordinary emphasis. "Shall I tell you the secret of the whole world? It is that we have only known the back of the world. We see everything from behind, and it looks brutal. That is not a tree, but the back of a tree. That is not a cloud, but the back of a cloud. Cannot you see that everything is stooping and hiding a face? If we could only get round in front...."[18]

3. PHILOSOPHIZING *IN MEDIAS RES*

There is a third common trait between poetry, philosophy and prayer. This one has to do, neither with their finality, nor with their object, but rather with their context. Here, even more than with the first two traits, G. K. Chesterton's message will strongly resound.

Let us start with poetry. There is in particular one feature of that grand type of poetry which furnished most of the education for a Greek schoolboy: the epic. The feature I mean is identified by Horace in his *Ars Poetica* as the requirement that a true epic begin *in medias res* ("placed in the midst of things"). Homer does not begin the *Odyssey* with his hero leaving Troy to return to Ithaca, but rather already on his way home—between his origin and destination—and reflecting poetically, "in the midst of things," on them both.

This feature is most evident in epic, but it is in a wider sense true of all genuine poetry. As Max Picard writes:

18. MT, 170.

> The poet makes poetry with the poetry that is given to him in advance. Poetry has an objective existence of its own. There is poetry in the world before man even begins to write poetry. Man responds to the poetry that comes to him by writing poetry of his own.[19]

The poet's response is precisely a response to a world already there. Likewise, the man of prayer already finds himself in the midst of a world and, indeed, in the midst of afflictions—then he prays.

This is true of philosophy too. Our modern innovators, following Descartes, try to cast off this exigency as a hindrance. A hindrance it is indeed—for those who aspire to think like God, rather than like a creature.

The world is already there, and, just as evidently, *our knowledge of it is already there.* If the philosopher does not begin as one who has been thrown "into the midst of things," he will sooner or later come to doubt whether there are any things to be in the midst of to begin with. This is the deadlock to which the Cartesian strategy sooner or later leads.

Now this beginning *in medias res* has need of poetry, to be sure. Before orderly philosophizing can commence, the philosopher's memory must be well supplied with the true-to-life images of the real, and have a rich experience of the concrete. The delight of poetry will lead him to that climax of wonder which, in turn, generates the philosophical question. But when once the philosopher has begun his proper work, he is confronted with the great temptation which Chesterton has already exposed; that is, he considers throwing off the basis of that poetic preparation, and pursuing a new and rationalized beginning.

Certainly the philosopher does not build his *arguments* on poetry, or use a "poetic method" in his procedure (despite

19. Picard, *Man and Language*, trans. by Stanley Goodman (Chicago: Gateway, 1963), 146.

the arbitrary miscegenations of some contemporary thinkers). But what he does do is introduce his reason into the foundation of all his songs, poems, and dances; for that foundation was the first encounter with being itself. Rather than devising a new point of departure and recasting his experience, the philosopher fares better by merely introducing the rational mode of discourse into the wealth of reality he already has experienced on the sensory and imaginative level. His logic will not be his foundation, but merely a new tool in knowing the already-encountered universe. Chesterton advises us as to the true use of the tool of logic:

> A great deal is said in these days about the value or valuelessness of logic. In the main, indeed, logic is not a productive tool so much as a weapon of defence. A man building up an intellectual system has to build like Nehemiah, with the sword in one hand and the trowel in the other. The imagination, the constructive quality, is the trowel, and argument is the sword.[20]

Even the lights of poetry are but imaginative refractions of the primal light of being. And that first light is gained from one's sensory encounter with the universe. It is the basis of poetry and the reflectively appropriated, but never newly grounded, foundation for all philosophy. It is the source of all "those profound intellectual passions that concern themselves with the ultimates of the universe; with the philosophy that is even prior to poetry."[21]

The fairy-tales Chesterton celebrates with such affection are themselves but playful registrations of that abiding amazement at the world's very existence:

> It is true that I believe in fairy-tales—in the sense that I marvel so much at what does exist that I am the readier to

20. VT, 113.
21. C, 112.

> admit what might. I understand the man who believes in the Sea Serpent on the ground that there are more fish in the sea than ever come out of it.[22]

That first salute of the universe enters into the mind and braces it with the idea of being, and in the same seizure, the world's marvelous transcendence over the little mind of man opens like a sky over a meadow. I remarked that perceived ignorance is the token of true wonder. It is only by holding on to that learned ignorance that anyone can be wise enough to wonder. To teach us this, old Socrates walked the earth like a natural messiah sent by the cosmos; he died, that the gates of earth might be opened to our fallen minds.

If we remain humble and happy as philosophers, we will one day learn the greatest lesson of all: that just as true poetry leads to philosophy, so does true philosophy lead to prayer. For us, poetry begins with delight and ends in wonder—but philosophy begins with wonder and ends in awe. Socrates ended his life writing a poem to a god. Aristotle, it is said, did much the same. The feather with which St. Thomas was penning the *Summa* seemed to be taken from his hand by an angel and stuck back into its wing; for the saint had stopped writing, and asked only to comment on *The Song of Songs*. Months later he was dead. Even Martin Heidegger turned at last from the plodding phenomenology of Husserl to the lyric poetry of Hölderlin. If we philosophize long and well, we may one day put down our books and build a church.

> The more we attempt to analyze that strange element of wonder, which is the soul of all the arts, the more we shall see that it must depend on some subordination of the self to a glory existing beyond it, and even in spite of it. Man always feels as a creature when he acts as a creator. When

22. OS, 9.

he carves a cathedral it is to make a monster that can swallow him.[23]

To attempt to make of philosophy a "strict science" is to take leave of all these lessons, and try one's own hand at creation. Well, history's verdict is already in: we are not very good at it. We may build little worlds we can understand, and they may be curious and efficient, but they will never be wonderful. And the worst fruit of our new productivity will be an inability to see even wonderful things in a wonder-struck way. Indeed, looking at our very own selves, our mind can easily get in the way (as it does with some evolutionists) and the sensory and imaginative shock of our make-up be tamed to a silly purr by misplaced reason.

> If the universe be taken piecemeal in the manner of the syllogist, it may be found that every detail and iota of man's origin and progress is accounted for and related to other facts. Looked at thus microscopically, man may be made to appear as common-place and mechanical as a larva or an amoeba; but looked at simply and suddenly, looked at in its whole bulk and proportion, the position of man in nature is a monstrous and miraculous thing.[24]

Babies still see things like this. Little children do too. They still see the world as a wonder and are still surprised by the stars. Of the children, Chesterton writes:

> As we walk the streets and see below us those delightful bulbous heads, three times too big for the body, which mark these human mushrooms, we ought always primarily to remember that within every one of these heads there is a new universe, as new as it was on the seventh day of creation.[25]

23. II, 213.
24. LL, 36.
25. DE, 149.

With poetry, with philosophy, and then with prayer, we are listening in three different ways to the whispered language of the universe. Whispered, because in our fallen world, human ears are too frail for the unmuffled decibels of the big bang of being. But in the midst of that useless, wonderful universe, we can slowly approach the wisdom that is one with humility, and the Beloved Who is greater than the lover, and Who longs to share a message that would be too fierce for us quite yet.

> But even in our quiet life I think we can feel the great fact that is the core of all religion. However quiet may be the skies, or however cool the meadows, we always feel that if we did know what they meant the meaning would be something mighty and shattering. About the weakest weed there is still a sensational difference between understanding and not understanding. We stare at a tree in an infinite leisure; but we know all the time that the real difference is between a stillness of mystery and an explosion of explanation.[26]

26. CM, 64.

By Way of Conclusion

In bringing this book to its end, it would be well to repeat in unmistakable language a point that was made in Part I. There it was remarked that rather than reading the books of Chesterton, the educated person should be able to go directly to Plato, Augustine, Aristotle and Aquinas, but that we are sadly unable to do so in our disjointed times. For this reason, it was maintained, Chesterton is important. He prepares us for the real philosophers by placing us at the beginning, in the midst of things, where first principles begin to brace the mind with the grasp of being. Now a final point that needs to be made is that although principles are indispensable to philosophy, we must not make the mistake of identifying them with philosophy. They are no more philosophy than a point is a line, a line a surface or a surface a solid.

Principles provide a platform for the launch of reason, but it is the launch that is important, not the launch-pad. Philosophy's proper work is indeed that of reason; wonder inspires and accompanies that work, but it does not constitute it. And if Chesterton has been called here a philosopher, it is not primarily because he reasons so well (and that he does), but rather because he illustrates so brilliantly the inalienable character of that which reason must presuppose, but can never prove. That is why he may be called in this special sense a philosopher, and not because he merits to be placed in the ranks of the immortals.

The first part of this book attempted to outline the peculiar character of Chesterton's philosophical propadeutic—brilliant in its illustration of the inner nature of principles in human knowing, dramatic in its depiction of the existential consequences our attitude to principles generates, and rhetorical, indeed journalistic (in the best senses of those words), in its ability to bring all this home to a 20th-century mind. Chesterton found the lessons of first principles to be preparations for philosophy and ultimately for Christian theology.

In the second part of the book we saw how the philosophical disorientation generated by Cartesianism and Kantianism derives not so much from their teachings as such, but from their beginnings. The failure of modern philosophy to produce a grand and successful new project of the philosophical enterprise was seen to be due to its failure to begin with evident, although pre-rational, points of departure. Anyone who has studied 20th-century philosophy in depth will have noticed how many trend-setting thinkers have crowned their careers by pronouncing funeral orations on philosophy. In their own way, they give witness to the truth that philosophy is doomed to a sad end if it commences with a bad beginning. As Thomas Aquinas once remarked: "(what seems to be) a small error at the beginning can become a huge error at the end."

In the third part of our book, Chesterton's *Orthodoxy* provided us with a hitherto unmatched dramatization of where first principles really stand in the whole business of thought. That position can only be energetically pointed out—and denials of it refuted—but cannot be demonstrated in terms of something more basic, because it is itself the basis of all else we know.

In the final part of the book, I have taken the liberty of identifying three conspicuous features of traditional, premodern philosophy, pointed out indeed, but never isolated and treated in their own right in the writings of Chesterton. Principles, and the universe they put us in the presence of, precede and transcend utility, establish and make possible the work of reason, and take us at once into the midst of a wealth of reality we find ourselves deeply involved with long before we learn to ask questions about it.

These crude building blocks of thought are laid down by Chesterton as the foundation stones for all philosophy. And the conclusion of our book is simply that these foundation stones are also touchstones, for their adamantine girding of the mind establishes forever the first fact we know: the world is there, and I have touched it.

APPENDIX

Appreciations of G.K. Chesterton

There can be no doubt that Chesterton's journalistic medium, along with his habitual playful manner, have made it difficult for many to appreciate the philosophical content of his writing, so emphasized in the present book. A few notable testimonies are therefore offered below, beginning with the now famous response of the Thomist, Etienne Gilson, upon reading Chesterton's rapidly written and hastily researched book on St. Thomas Aquinas:

Etienne Gilson:

> "I am envious of Chesterton and disgusted with myself. I have taught Aquinas for years, but I simply could not write that book. How did Chesterton manage to do it? He has not devoted himself to the study of philosophy, nor has he written other books on philosophy which might point the way to this astonishing one. Nevertheless, he has in this book penetrated to the heart of problems which philosophers have been trying to clarify for years. Only a man of extraordinary philosophical insight could do this."[1]

Asked after Chesterton's death to elaborate, Gilson responded:

> "I consider it as being without possible comparison the best book ever written on St. Thomas. Nothing short of genius can account for such an achievement. Everybody will no doubt admit that it is a 'clever' book, but the few

1. E.J.M. McCorkell, *Memoirs* (Toronto, 1975), 78.

readers who have spent twenty or thirty years in studying St. Thomas Aquinas, and who, perhaps, have themselves published two or three volumes on the subject, cannot fail to perceive that the so-called 'wit' of Chesterton has put their scholarship to shame. He has guessed all that which they had tried to demonstrate, and he has said all that which they were more or less clumsily attempting to express in academic formulas. Chesterton was one of the deepest thinkers who ever existed; he was deep because he was right; and he could not help being right; but he could not either help being modest and charitable, so he left it to those who could understand him to know that he was right, and deep; to the others, he apologized for being right, and he made up for being deep by being witty. That is all they can see of him."[2]

Reflection and time only confirmed Gilson's judgment, for thirty years after the above assessment, he wrote: Chesterton was "nearer the real Thomas than I am after reading and teaching the Angelic Doctor for sixty years."[3]

T. S. Eliot:

"If I were to state his essential quality, I would say that it is a sort of triumphant common sense—that *gaudium de veritate*, of which philosophers discourse—a joyous acclaim toward the splendor and the powers of the soul...."[4]

Paul Claudel:

"To judge Chesterton on his 'contributions to literature,' then, would be to apply the wrong standards of measure-

2. Maisie Ward, *Gilbert Keith Chesterton* (New York: Sheed & Ward, 1953), 620.

3. Gilson, in letter to Fr. Kenneth Scanell, January 7, 1966, in Lynette Hunter, *G.K. Chesterton: Explorations in Allegory* (London: Macmillan, 1979), 173.

4. Eliot's "Obituary Note" in *The Tablet*, June 20, 1936, 785.

ment. It is in other matters that he was importantly and consistently on the side of the angels. . . ."[5]

George Bernard Shaw:

"...a colossal genius..."[6]

Fr. Vincent McNabb:

"Chesterton's mind, so essentially philosophical, recognized that if a being is related to the Absolute, that relation is its absolute relation. It was not just the poet in him, it was first of all the philosopher in him that, when he walked the fields, saw in the daisy the eye of God, and, when he sauntered abstractedly down the Strand, saw a ladder stretching from heaven to Charing Cross. . . . There is hardly a line of his writings that does not say to me with emphasis: 'This man is a philosopher'. But there are few if any lines that do not say with equal emphasis; 'This philosopher is a poet.'"[7]

Hilaire Belloc:

"Truth had for him the immediate attraction of an appetite. He was hungry for reality. But what is much more, he could not conceive of himself except as satisfying that hunger; it was not possible for him to hesitate in the acceptance of each new parcel of truth; it was not possible for him to hold anything worth holding that was not connected with the truth as a whole. . . . It would have been better, perhaps, had he never fallen into verbalism (wherein he tended to

5. Claudel's letter of salutation to the Crusader G.K.C. at Holy Cross, USA., November 11, 1930, in booklet *Mr. Chesterton at Holy Cross*, honoring the author's visit to Holy Cross College, Massachusetts.

6. Maisie Ward, *Return to Chesterton* (New York: Sheed & Ward, 1952), 4.

7. "Gilbert Keith Chesterton" in *A Vincent McNabb Anthology*, ed. Francis E. Nugent (London, 1955), 85–86.

exceed). For fools were led thereby to think that he was merely verbalist whereas he was in reality a thinker so profound and so direct that he had no equal. . . . [He had a] precision of thought and supreme talent for exact logic. . . . One effect of Chesterton's unique and exceptional precision of thought is the peculiar satisfaction his writing gives to men of philosophical training or instinct. . . .

"The heart of his style is lucidity, produced by a complete rejection of ambiguity: complete exactitude of definition. . . . His mind was oceanic, subject indeed to a certain restriction of repeated phrase and manner, but in no way restricted as to the action of the mind. He swooped upon an idea like an eagle, tore it with active beak into its constituent parts and brought out the heart of it. If ever a man analyzed finally and conclusively, Chesterton did so. . . . There was no other writer of our time in whom the appeal to the reader was perpetually through the intelligence."[8]

Ronald Knox:

"There are only a few whose thought seems to spring out of them clothed in words that adequately express it: Plato, for example, or Pascal. Chesterton was an artist in thought. He was an artist in the sense of one who drew pictures, before he started writing; and most of us know how, in his pictures, a single figure, full of movement, stands out luminous from a vague background. So his mind saw things; it seized instinctively on the essences of them. . . .

"I call that man intellectually great, who sees the whole of life as a coherent system; who can touch on any theme,

8. Hilaire Belloc, "Gilbert Keith Chesterton," *Saturday Review of Literature*, XIV, July 4, 1936, 4; and *On the Place of Gilbert Chesterton in English Letters* (Patmos, West Virginia, 1977), 55, 57–58, 91–99, and "It Was a Benediction to Know Him," *The Universe*, June 19, 1936, 11.

and illuminate it, and always in a way that is related to the rest of his thought, so that you say, 'Nobody but he would have written that.' Chesterton was such a man."[9]

C. S. Lewis:

"His humor was of the kind which I like best—not 'jokes' embedded in the page like currants in a cake, still less (what I cannot endure), a general tone of flippancy and jocularity, but is rather (as Aristotle would say) the 'bloom' on dialectic itself. The sword glitters not because the swordsman set out to make it glitter but because he is fighting for his life and therefore moving it very quickly. For the critics who think Chesterton frivolous or 'paradoxical' I have to work hard to feel even pity; sympathy is out of the question. Moreover, strange as it may seem, I liked him for his goodness."[10]

Joseph de Tonquédec:

"And when, after having abundantly criticized, bantered and upset everyone, he finally consents to tell us what he himself thinks, a philosophy issues forth quite naturally from his pen, which, once perceived, can be followed in its latent circulation through his entire opus. . . . He insists on being treated as a philosopher, and we have seen how he invites us—I almost said provokes us—to the discussion of ideas."[11]

Frank Sheed:

"This man of all seasons was a rare combination, perhaps a unique combination, of humorous jester and profound

9. Ronald Knox, June 18, 1941, cited in *Chesterton Review*, vol. 2, Spring–Summer 1979, 302.

10. C.S. Lewis, *Surprised by Joy* (New York: Fount Paperbacks, 1982), 53.

11. Joseph Tonquédec, *G.K. Chesterton, ses idées et son charactère* (Paris, 1926), 8, 27 (my translation).

philosopher. I think that in all the history of philosophy there has never been a philosopher who played the jester, the fool, so outrageously. Nor has there ever been a jester who had any ideas to compare with those of Chesterton....

"He didn't just concentrate on a particular area. In a way, he saw everything at once.... He lived in the totality. His mind would move about the totality very surprisingly, jumping from the unimportant or the casual to the very heart of reality, jumping to the periphery and then jumping back again.... One of the most extraordinary things... [was that] he very seldom repeats himself.... *This extraordinary power of seeing what he looked at*, and more and more that mind of his was looking into the totality—he never sees anything without seeing everything—made him the philosopher."[12] [emphasis added]

Graham Greene:

"Much of the difficulty of theology arises from the efforts of men who are not primarily writers to distinguish a quite simple idea with the utmost accuracy. [Chesterton] restated the original thought with the freshness, simplicity, and excitement of discovery. In fact, it was discovery: he unearthed the defined from beneath the definitions, and the reader wondered why the definitions had ever been thought necessary."[13]

Marshall McLuhan:

"[Chesterton's] profound humility in the face of reality... is the reason for [his] energetic revival of tradition in so far as it dignifies and illuminates any present

12. Frank Sheed, "Chesterton in All Seasons," in *A Chesterton Celebration*, ed. R.W. Rauch (Notre Dame, 1983), 52, 59–60.

13. Graham Greene, "G.K. Chesterton" in *Collected Essays* (London, 1969), 136–37.

activity. In short, he is original in the only possible sense, because he considers everything in relation to its origin. He was a Thomist by connaturality with being, not by study of St. Thomas ... he seems never to have reached any position by dialectic or doctrine, but to have enjoyed a kind of connaturality with every kind of reasonableness."[14]

Ralph McInerny:

"I propose to [call him a philosopher], and to suggest that there may be something salutary for philosophy in so regarding him.... I will tolerate any objection predicated on the assumption that calling Chesterton a philosopher puts him in low company. What I should resist is any suggestion that he does not quite make the grade. [McInerny then quotes from the little book Belloc had written on G.K., which we have already cited:]

Now parallelism is a gift or method of vast effect in the conveyance of truth. Parallelism consists in the illustration of some unperceived truth by its exact consonance with the reflection of a truth already known and perceived. A truth may be missed by too constant a use, so that familiarity has dulled it; or by mere lack of acquaintance with it (the opposite danger); or by the repeated statement of it in false and imperfect forms. When the truth has been missed, it is recalled and fixed in the mind of the hearer by an unexpected and vivid use of parallelism.

Out of this passage I believe, one can bring forth all that is needed to justify dubbing Chesterton a philosopher.... His puns and word-play, his gift of parallelism, all have the ability to induce the shock of recognition.

Both Plato and Aristotle assure us that philosophy begins in wonder and ends in awe. It starts with a puzzle,

14. In *Chesterton Review*, February, 1984, vol. X, no. 1, 83, and McLuhan's introduction to Hugh Kenner's *Paradox in Chesterton* (New York: Sheed and Ward, 1947), xii, xix.

continues with inquiry and argument and definition, but is fulfilled in contemplation. Taken in that broad sense of the activity, it is inevitable that we should see Chesterton as a kind of philosopher, a popular kind perhaps, but one who is constantly making us see what is right before our nose."[15]

15. Ralph McInerny, "Chesterton as Peeping Thomist" from *A Chesterton Celebration*, 9, 17–18; where he quotes Belloc, *On the Place…*, 60–61.

Bibliography

Chesterton's Works Cited in This Book

Below is an alphabetical listing of the titles and editions of the works of Chesterton that are quoted or referred to in this book. They are preceded by the abbreviations used in the notes. *Orthodoxy* is not included, as it is the focus of the study, and has appeared in multiple editions; the numerous quotes from that book in Part III are not referenced according to the pagination of any edition, but are always taken from the corresponding chapter under discussion.

AB *Autobiography*, New York: Sheed and Ward, 1936.

ACD *Appreciations and Criticisms of the Works of Charles Dickens*, London: J. M. Dent and Sons, 1911.

AS *All I Survey*, New York: Dodd, Mead and Co., 1933.

CD *Charles Dickens*, New York: Dodd, Mead and Co., 1909.

CL *Coloured Lands*, New York: Sheed and Ward, 1938.

CM *The Common Man*, New York: Sheed and Ward, 1950.

CW *Collected Works*, Ignatius Press, San Francisco, 1986–.

DE *The Defendant*, London: J. M. Dent & Sons, 1901.

EM *The Everlasting Man*, Garden City: Image Books, 1955.

FA *St. Francis of Assisi*, Garden City: Image Books, 1957.

FF *Fancies versus Fads*, London: Methuen & Co., 1923.

GS *Generally Speaking*, New York: Dodd, Mead and Co., 1929 (reprint: Freeport, NY: Books for Libraries Press, 1969).

H *Heretics*, New York: John Lane Co., 1919.

II *Irish Impressions*, New York: John Lane Co., 1919.

IN *The Innocence of Fr. Brown*, Harmondsworth: Penguin Books, 1950.

LL *Lunacy and Letters*, New York: Sheed and Ward, 1958.

MAN *Manalive*, New York: John Lane Co., 1912.

NJ *The New Jerusalem*, London: Hodder and Stoughton, 1921.

O *Orthodoxy*, Garden City: Image Books, 1959.

OS *Outline of Sanity*, Blackrock, Ireland: Carraig Books, 1928.

PL *The Poet and the Lunatics*, New York: Dodd, Mead and Co., 1937.

RR *Resurrection of Rome*, London: Hodder and Stoughton, 1934.

SS *Superstitions of the Sceptic*, Cambridge: Darwen Finlayson, 1964.

TA *St. Thomas Aquinas*, New York: Image Books, 1956.

UD *Uses of Diversity*, London: Methuen & Co., 1920.

VT *Varied Types*, New York: Dodd, Mead and Co., 1903 (reprint: Freeport, NY: Books for Libraries Press, 1968).

WB *William Blake*, London: Duckworth & Co., 1910.

WW *What's Wrong with the World*, New York: Dodd, Mead and Co., 1910 (reprint: Peru, IL: Sherwood Sugden & Co.).

About the Author

SCOTT RANDALL PAINE is a priest of the archdiocese of Brasilia, and professor of Medieval Philosophy and Oriental Thought at the University of Brasilia. A native of the United States, since 1974 he has lived, studied, and taught in various countries of Europe, Asia, and South America. He has published widely in both Portuguese and English on religious and philosophical topics, including most recently an anthology of the works of the British philosopher, Bernard Kelly (Angelico Press, 2017). He has been Visiting Scholar at Munich's Hochschule für Philosophie, the National University of Singapore and Harvard Divinity School. His current writing and research can be followed at disciplinedwonder.com.

Made in the USA
Coppell, TX
13 December 2019

12864886R00143